THE MULCH BOOK

A Complete Guide for Gardeners

by Stu Campbell

Revised and updated
by Donna Moore

A Down-to-Earth Book

Storey Books
Schoolhouse Road
Pownal, Vermont 05261

The mission of Storey Communications is to serve our customers
by publishing practical information that encourages personal independence
in harmony with the environment.

Cover illustration by Alison Kolesar
Interior illustrations by Carl Kirkpatrick
Cover and text design by Wanda Harper

Copyright © 1991 by Storey Communications, Inc.

Storey Publishing books are available for special premium and promotional uses and for customized editions. For further information, please call the Custom Publishing Department at 1-800-793-9396.

Printed in the United States by R.R. Donnelley
20 19 18 17 16 15 14 13 12 11

Library of Congress Cataloging-in-Publication Data

Campbell, Stu.
    The mulch book : a complete guide for gardeners / Stu Campbell. — Rev. and updated
/ by Donna Moore.
        p.   cm. — (A Down-to-earth book)
    Includes index.
    ISBN 0-88266-659-2 (pb)
    1. Mulching.   2. Vegetable gardening.   3. Fruit-culture.   I. Moore, Donna, 1958-
    II. Title.   III. Series.
S661.5.C35   1991
635.04—dc20
                                                                90-50603
                                                                CIP

Contents

To Cricket
*May she not be thirty
before she has a garden all her own.*

Preface

Mulching first began to appeal to me when I realized that it might save me and my family some work. You see, I detest hand weeding. That may be an admission that any so-called "gardener" should never make. I think it is because I had to do so much of it in my mother's large garden as a boy. Because I justifiably could not be trusted to, my mother did all of the interesting stuff like planting, staking, and picking. The hot, repetitious gnome's work was relegated to me. And you know, an amazingly large number of my friends who are still turned off by gardening have similar horrifying memories—however accurate or inaccurate they may be—of acres and acres of witchgrass to be pulled, row upon row of corn to be cultivated. If I am honest with myself, I realize that I actually did very little weeding and a great deal of complaining about it.

Whether or not mulching actually *does* save you work—when you consider the number of calories expended to build a garden as compared to the number of calories you take out of it—has never been accurately documented so far as I know. But I like to think that it does. It *surely* saves you a lot of time that you would have had to spend cultivating and weeding. In fact, the nicest thing about mulching, when you come right down to it, is that if you mulch, your *children* may not have to do so much monotonous work in the garden.

This leads me to the first point of *The Mulch Book:* We cannot allow our children to be turned off by gardening. Don't children learn better if their drudgery is reduced? It is they, after all, who must learn—and teach their children—to grow food for themselves, to make use of materials sparingly and wisely, and to give back to the precious land at least some, if not all, of what they take from it.

I feel in my own case that I should try to keep history from repeating itself. But in spite of my efforts to make gardening less work for my family by mulching, I am as guilty as the next parent when it comes to turning my children off. Our three-year-old daughter comes wandering into the garden when I am there, overflowing with questions, eager to explore, bursting with helpfulness. My delight at seeing her there nearly mirrors the fascination in her eyes. But soon I am preoccupied and slightly impatient with her persistent questions. I answer her inadequately. I worry about her stepping on things. I am anguished that her stubby fingers can't spread carrot seeds evenly enough. So she drifts sadly away to find something or someone more interesting. I worry that the garden has lost her.

The second point is this: After months of studying the intricacies of mulching, the temptation is to think of mulch as the panacea for all gardening ills. *It is not.* As one old gardener cautioned me, mulching is just one arrow in the gardener's quiver. All of us— gardeners as well as the other unfortunate nongardening individuals who also happen to inhabit our planet—have to retain a sense of perspective. Gardening is like anything else. We can get so bogged down with "the way we've always done it" that we never permit the gardening part of ourselves to grow in the same way we hope our gardens will. On the other hand, wise and confident gardeners know enough to guard against fads. Instead of scurrying off to buy and try the latest thing, they take a long, close look to see if it will, in fact, benefit their particular situation.

I want you to remember as you are reading *The Mulch Book* that mulching is only a part of gardening. It is not the whole story. *The Mulch Book* is only one brief chapter in the tremendous body of scientific information, practical experience, literature, and folklore that would comprise the "Complete Gardening Book," which because of its vast nature can never be fully written.

In the final analysis, to anticipate the book a little for you before you even begin, mulching is like a double-headed axe. It is a useful tool, but it can be a dangerous one if not used carefully. In most cases, mulching should be used like an insurance policy, as a way of hedging your bet on the success of your garden. Ideally we should have large enough gardens, all of us, so that we could mulch part of each crop—guarding it against drought, weeds, and heat—and leave the other part without mulch. By not going whole hog, either way, in any given year, we would all at least come up with something to eat.

Charlotte, Vermont   Fall, 1973

Chapter 1

Introduction

T*he Mulch Book* was originally written in the early 1970s, when interest in vegetable gardening was peaking. At that time, the most celebrated benefit of mulching was that it reduced or eliminated time spent weeding the vegetable garden. While that advantage still holds, mulching has become an even greater factor in the area of water conservation.

Our water supply is finite and often unevenly distributed. Some gardeners may be suffering from water shortages and brush fires, while others are building levees and raised beds. Although mulches may not do much to control excess moisture, they are essential in the battle against water loss.

They are so important, in fact, that in 1989 a bill was introduced in California that, among other things, required the use of mulches. This bill has often been referred to as the Xeriscape Act of 1989. Before you think I'm using dirty words, let me explain. *Xeriscaping* is a relatively new garden design principle whose aim is to reduce the amount of water used on landscapes. While the idea of conserving water in the garden has been around for some time, the xeriscape concept was refined by the Denver Water Department in 1981, after a particularly dry summer. They developed what have become the seven basic principles of xeriscaping: proper planning and design, limited use of turf areas, use of efficient irrigation systems, soil improvements, *mulching,* use of plants that demand less water, and appropriate maintenance (weeding, fertilizing, etc.). This concept quickly spread to Florida, Texas, Arizona, and California, where droughts are a fact of life. The National Xeriscaping Council, Inc. has also been established in Austin, Texas to coordinate and promote the xeriscaping movement. After all that, who would need to be convinced to use mulches?

It seems, though, that mulching does deserve more justification. For one thing, *mulch* doesn't even *sound* very nice, which may be one strike against it to begin with. In its earliest Middle English sense the word "mulsh" was an adjective that meant, according to Mr. Webster, "soft or yielding." That's not so bad. But by the time our language had evolved into what is now called Early Modern English centuries later, the "s" in *mulsh* had become a "c," the adjective had become a noun, the word itself had come to mean "rotten hay," and something pleasant was lost in the evolution.

Now this is not to suggest that "rotten hay" is *necessarily* undesirable nor that rotted hay is the only kind of mulch there is. There are many, many kinds of materials that can be used for mulching, as we shall see. In fact, if you use your imagination a bit

A neatly mulched garden can bring many rewards.

you probably can dream up some things to use for mulch that are not mentioned in *The Mulch Book*. The point is that to the layman the thought of hoarding, handling, and spreading around heaps of old, dark, moldy hay at best is strange, not to say repulsive. To the knowledgeable gardener, on the other hand, mulch can be the most beautiful stuff in the world.

But mulching needs justification among serious and experienced gardeners, too. It is awfully hard to imagine at first glance that a subject like mulching could be very controversial. I mean, either you like to mulch your garden or you don't, right? Not so. Highly regarded gardening authorities like Ruth Stout, known to many gardeners as the "complete mulcher," and Leonard Wickenden, a prominent biochemist and thoroughly experienced organic gardener, have carried on a mulching debate in gardening literature for years. Some people don't know with whom to side, so they don't bother to mulch at all. We'll have a look at each of their points of view a little later on.

Some object to mulching for purely aesthetic reasons. Lots of gardeners prefer the traditional look of arrow-straight rows and bare, immaculately cultivated earth. There still are plenty of these "model" gardens around, and that sort of thing is fine if you have lots of time and patience, plenty of water, and maybe a few slave laborers around your house who can help you maintain this kind of elegance. Most of us do not. Let's face it: except for the very affluent, the days of the full-time hired gardener are gone forever. Besides, mulch does not *have* to be unattractive, as we shall also see.

Because my garden is here in a northern sector of the country, I know that what works well *specifically* for me may not necessarily work well for you in your garden. You also should remember that there is no one "right" way and no one "wrong" way to mulch. There are good ways and there are not-so-good ways. This book offers suggestions about *some* ways to mulch your gardens to make them happier, healthier, and more rewarding. I will also try to make you aware of certain dangers and pitfalls, but I will never say, "This is *the* way." That is for you to decide.

Chapter 2

Here's Why: The Benefits of Mulching

M ulching has many benefits, not the least of which, as far as I'm concerned, is that you can walk around in your garden on rainy days and not have three inches of sticky mud on the soles of your shoes when you come back inside. I choose to ignore the experts' warnings about staying completely out of the garden on wet days. I am careful not to touch anything, mindful that I might be transmitting some harmful bacteria or virus to the plants. And I try to stay in the middle of my mulched path so I don't compact the soil near my plants. But it seems to be a compulsive ritual with me to go into my garden at least once a day. I need to squat down next to a row and gently (sometimes not so gently) try to coax young seedlings into growing faster, bigger, or greener. Not a scientific argument for mulching, I know, but certainly an emotional one.

For the more technical benefits of mulching I turned to Dr. Donald Rakow, Professor of Landscape Horticulture at Cornell University. According to Dr. Rakow, the three major benefits of mulch are: the reduction of water losses from the soil, the suppression of weed growth, and the protection from soil temperature extremes.

Soil Moisture Retention
Mulch's ability to conserve soil moisture has long been documented. It may be its most universally recognized virtue. While authorities and test results differ, it is clear that moisture evaporation from soil covered with mulch is reduced anywhere from 10 to 50 percent.

Whichever you accept, the water-conserving value of mulching can't be overemphasized, especially in these times of water restrictions and shortages.

Mulch keeps the soil from drying out partly because it prevents dew and water, drawn up from the subsoil, from escaping. Contrary to what a lot of people believe, dew is not only condensation of water from the atmosphere, it is also condensation of moisture from the air pockets found in the soil. Most dew is completely wasted, as far as plant growth is concerned, unless there is something on the surface to catch it and prevent it from evaporating.

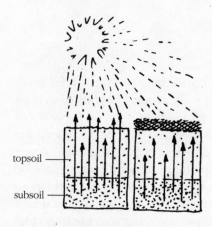

topsoil

subsoil

Mulch keeps the soil from drying out because it inhibits evaporation of dew and moisture, which is drawn up from the subsoil by capillary action.

Some impervious mulches like black plastic, aluminum foil, or old boards may catch more of the dew because they don't allow air to pass through. While these types of mulches won't let the dew out, they also don't let water or air in. Something to keep in mind when selecting a mulch. More on that later.

Weed Suppression

As for weed control, Dr. Rakow explained, one study has found weeding time to be reduced by almost two-thirds through the use of mulches. Mulching can practically eliminate the need for weeding and cultivating. Imagine how much extra time that will leave you for picking strawberries or lying in the hammock!

There are a few catches, however. First, the mulch itself must be weed-free. Many a gardener has had the best mulching intentions go

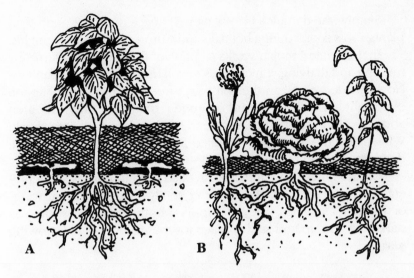

If the mulch is deep enough (A) weeds will come up in darkness and wither away. If a mulch is too thin (B) some weeds will poke themselves through. Even when this is the case they are easy to spot and easy to pull.

astray with one application of weed-strewn hay or manure. They ended up introducing more weeds to their garden than they controlled.

Second, a mulch must be deep enough to prevent existing weed seeds from germinating. As with most other seeds, weeds need light to germinate. Those weeds trying to come up under a mulch come up in darkness and wither away. If a mulch is applied too thinly or unevenly, weeds may still find their way through. So when applying your mulch, you'll want to think like a weed and cover all the open areas.

Finally, mulches won't smother all weeds. Some particularly tough weeds have the fortitude to push themselves up through just about any mulch. These should be easy to spot, however, and even more easily plucked when growing in a mulched bed.

Soil Temperature

The effect mulching has on soil temperatures is probably one of the most often overlooked benefits, especially by first-time gardeners. Many of us are more concerned with aboveground temperatures and don't spend much time pondering what's happening underground.

Simply stated, mulch is insulation. It keeps the soil around your plants' roots cooler during hot days and warmer during cooler nights.

In the winter, mulch works to prevent the soil from alternately freezing and thawing, which leads to soil heaving and root damage. Now this doesn't mean the soil won't freeze; it just won't happen overnight. It's those rapid changes that not only threaten aboveground growth, but may send tender plant roots into shock. Winter mulches are usually applied in the fall, after the plants are dormant, and are removed the following spring.

On the other hand, mulches are also used to control soil temperatures in the summer. These are frequently referred to as "growing" or "cultural" mulches. They are applied in the spring after the soil starts to warm up and stay in place for the majority of the growing season.

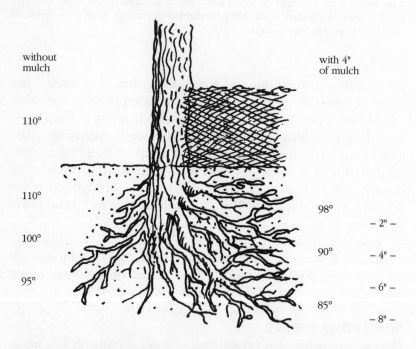

without mulch

with 4" of mulch

110°

110°

98°

— 2" —

100°

90°

— 4" —

95°

— 6" —

85°

— 8" —

Mulch is insulation. It keeps the soil around your plants' roots cooler during hot days and warmer during cooler nights. The roots of a newly transplanted raspberry cane, for example, will die on a very hot day if the soil temperature is allowed to rise much above 100 degrees F.

In some cases, the purpose may be to raise the soil temperature—when you're using black plastic around tomatoes and peppers, for example. In others, mulch may be applied to keep the soil temperatures down. Extremely high soil temperatures can inhibit root growth and may actually damage some shallow-rooted plants. During those long, hot days of summer, a mulch can reduce soil temperature by as much as 10 degrees F.

Growing mulches can be partially or entirely removed at the end of the season. Most of the organic types are usually incorporated right into the soil. Which leads us to some of the other benefits gained by mulching.

Stabilizes and Improves the Soil

Mulching prevents soil compaction and crusting of the soil surface by absorbing the impact of falling raindrops. Water penetrates through loose, granulated soil but runs off hard, compacted earth. Mulch will control wind and water erosion by slowing water runoff and will help to hold soil in place, even on steep slopes. This is why we see newly grassed banks along highways covered with mulch. It keeps the dust down, too.

Mulch can be considered a soil conditioner. Some soils, which might normally break up into chunks when tilled or cultivated, will crumble into fine granules after even just a few weeks under a mulch.

Many of the organic mulches, like shredded leaves or bark chips, will add organic matter to your soil as they decompose. This additional organic matter leads to all sorts of great things. Soil structure is enhanced, which improves aeration, water percolation, and nutrient movement through your soil.

Mulching will also encourage the presence of earthworms, which further aerate the soil and release nutrients in the form of "castings." Earthworms should be considered prominent citizens in any garden and are particularly important in perennial beds or in garden plots that are rarely plowed or tilled. Mulching keeps your soil friable without your having to work at it.

Mulch stimulates increased microbial activity in the soil. Certain bacteria are every bit as important as worms. The result of their work is that organic matter breaks down more rapidly and plant nutrients are made available to your plants sooner. This means, as Ruth Stout suggests, that your garden is operating very much like a compost heap.

Helps You Grow Healthier Plants

Mulched plants, especially vegetables, are less diseased and more uniform than those without mulch. One reason is that mulching prevents fruits, flowers, and other plant parts from being splashed by mud and water during heavy rains. Not only can this splashing lead to unsightly spots and messy fruit, it is one of the primary means of infection for many soil-borne diseases. Mulching protects ripening vegetables, like tomatoes, melons, pumpkins, and squash, from coming in direct contact with the soil, which means fewer "bad" spots, rotten places, and mold.

Although the jury is still out on whether mulches can help control harmful soil nematodes or fungi, there is some evidence that a few of the light-reflective types, such as aluminum foil or polyethylene film, may reduce aphid and leaf miner populations and some of the diseases spread by them.

Basically, mulching helps reduce plant stress. And, as many gardeners have said, healthy, strong plants tend to be bothered less by insects and other pests.

Nutrient Availability

Organic mulch can contribute to the potassium availability of a soil by allowing the potassium to latch on to the decaying mulch instead of the soil particles. Once fixed to the soil particles, a good deal of the potassium becomes unavailable to the plant.

Depending on their age, type, and length of exposure, mulches can also contribute nitrogen, phosphorus, and several trace elements to the soil chemistry.

As for their dependability, Dr. Rakow suggests supplementing mulched areas with some other fertilizer source, since the mulch alone may not be enough. Herbaceous plantings may actually show signs of chlorosis without an additional feeding or two.

Environmentally Sound

Using mulches for weed control helps cut down our use and dependence on chemical herbicides. The fewer chemicals we use, the lower the risk of ground water contamination and accidental poisonings.

Mulching is an excellent way to reduce and recycle yard waste. Even if you live on a quarter acre of land and have a small garden, you generate tremendous amounts of waste in and around your home. Rather than burning it or carting it off to a landfill, use it up! Dead plants, leaves, grass clippings, old newspapers—just about anything is fair game for the mulch pile. Even most of the larger woody materials can now be converted into mulch with one of those portable choppers or shredders. You can help your plants and the environment at the same time.

Appearance

Again, not one of the most scientific of reasons, but many folks mulch just because they like the way it looks. Ask your friends why they mulch. I'll bet they won't say "to free up my soil potassium." They will probably say mulching makes their garden look a little better or neater. Or maybe they just like the color or texture a certain mulch lends to their landscape.

Whatever your reason, mulching is a good idea. The hardest part, believe it or not, is putting it down in the first place. Hopefully, a few of the benefits listed above will be enough motivation for you to get out there and do it.

Chapter 3

To Give the Devils Their Due: Some Drawbacks to Mulching

Before you rush out and start mulching the neighborhood, I thought I'd introduce you to a few of the controversies associated with mulching. Mulching is not a new phenomenon and neither is arguing about it. For example, it must be more than forty years ago now that on a chilly spring morning a lady in Connecticut named Ruth Stout, who had both a very green thumb and a way with words, wandered into her garden and felt the ever-so-faint stirrings beneath her feet that only people who are attuned to such things can feel. Little did she know at that point, I would guess, that right then and there, as the seeds of three famous gardening books *(How to Have a Green Thumb without an Aching Back, Gardening without Work,* and *The No-Work Garden Book)* began to germinate in the fertility of her mind, that single-handedly she was about to revive and popularize the ancient art of mulching.

She wrote,

> . . . I was, as usual, trying to be patient until someone could do some plowing for me, when finally one day, I used my head. No, not for plowing—for reasoning. My asparagus was doing beautifully and I said to myself: that ground hasn't been plowed for over ten years; what has asparagus got that peas haven't? To heck with plowing! I'm going to plant . . .[1]

13

She started with the original mulch: hay—lots of it. Later Ruth Stout was to say,

> . . . After putting hay all over the garden I soon found that the only jobs left were planting, thinning, and picking. Whenever I wanted to put in some seeds, I raked the mulch back and planted, and later, when the seeds had sprouted, I pulled the mulch close around the little plants, thus keeping them moist and outwitting the weeds. . . .
>
> . . . My plot has become so rich now that I can plant very closely, and I don't even use manure or (chemical) fertilizer. The garden is one-eighth its original size and so luxuriant that in the fall we call it the jungle. . . .[2]

The Stout System

The Stout complete-mulching system is very simple. She was really a sheet-composter who used no machinery. "Make your garden your compost pile," she says. "My way is simply to keep a thick mulch of

This experiment, made at Garden Way years ago, verified Ruth Stout's theories about mulch on top of sod. Thick books of hay were laid on a plot of grass in the fall. In the spring plantings could be — and were — made there. The soil was moist and soft, and needed only to be scuffed with a hoe and rake. No plowing or tilling had to be done.

any vegetable matter that rots on both my garden and flower garden all year round."[3] A compost heap is too much trouble, she says. Just spread mulch where you eventually would have spread the compost anyway. In time it will rot and become rich dirt. In fact, she would go so far as to say that if you were to cover *sod* with a heavy layer of mulch in the fall, you could make plantings there—without plowing, tilling, or spading of any kind—the following spring.

> For the past twenty-six years I have used no fertilizer of any kind on any part of my garden except rotting mulch and cottonseed meal. I broadcast the latter in the winter at the rate of five pounds to every one hundred square feet of my plot. I'm not really convinced that my soil needs the meal, but I have been told it does for nitrogen.
>
> However, if gardeners weren't driving in here quite often to inspect my system, I think I would skip the cottonseed meal for a season and see if it made any difference. But as long as I am exhibiting the excellent results which I get from my method, with so little work, I can't afford to have a failure.[4]

Ruth Stout represents a charming antithesis to the kind of quasi-scientific approach to vegetable gardening that spewed reams of complicated, pamphletized data and contradictory advice from various headquarters of state university extension services throughout the country during the late forties and fifties.

She often leaves herself wide open to the criticism that she oversimplifies. Perhaps she does, but her reassuring advice to the neophyte gardener who is faced with the apparent complexities of mulching would be: *don't worry about it!* What about hay seeds in the mulch, you ask? If the mulch is thick enough, she would answer, the weeds won't come through. When do you start mulching, then, you might counter? "*Any* time!"

The Attack

Along came Leonard Wickenden, the "gardener's organic gardener," who didn't buy Ruth Stout's act. In his encyclopedic *Gardening with Nature,* where he relies heavily on his own scientific background, on his immense horticultural experiences, *and* on his own intuitive organic gardening sense, he jumps on mulching with both feet. He writes, in only slightly veiled reference to Mrs. Stout:

> Here we have a practice that has gained greatly in popularity in recent years . . . The soil between rows of crops is covered with a layer of straw, coarse hay, sawdust or trash of some kind. It is claimed for this practice that it retains moisture by checking evaporation, keeps down weeds, prevents undue baking of the soil and encourages the growth of earthworms. There is much truth in these claims. Weeds are by no means entirely eliminated, but those that make their way through the mulch are easily uprooted. Evaporation is checked and the soil kept cool, which means that earthworms will remain nearer the surface, although it does not necessarily follow that their numbers will increase.

> But there is another side of the picture. *If soil is covered by let us say coarse hay, much of any rain that falls on it will be held by the hay.* Since this rain will be spread in a thin film over the fibers, it will evaporate readily and the soil below will never get the benefit of it. In other words, whatever may be gained by retaining moisture already in the ground may be counterbalanced by what is lost in the subsequent rainfall.

> It is also a question whether the protection of the soil is entirely beneficial. Certainly in the spring every gardener longs for the warm sunshine to raise the temperature of his soil and so speed up the growth of his seedlings. *At what point do we decide the soil is getting too much warmth?*

> Finally, *there is the danger that natural forces and conditions will start converting the mulch into sheet compost; . . . this is likely to rob the soil of nitrogen.* It is particularly likely to occur in a wet season when both the mulch and soil in contact with it are continuously damp and thus favorable to the growth of microorganisms.

Mr. Wickenden concludes,

> . . . The advantages and disadvantages of mulching depend on the climate of the location and the weather of

the season. If a mulch could be applied at the beginning of a dry spell and removed at the beginning of a wet one, its value could probably be great. Since that is impracticable there is no clear indication of its value and the matter becomes one of personal judgement.[5]

The Rebuttal

Ruth Stout counters in *Gardening without Work*, "He (Leonard Wickenden) admits that he had never mulched his garden, yet he goes bravely ahead and explains what's 'wrong' with the idea." Her rebuttal is characteristically unscientific:

> He says, "Weeds are by no means entirely eliminated," which is misleading, for he certainly gives the impression that he is talking about all, or at least most weeds. The fact is that if you mulch deeply enough all weeds are eliminated except a few perennials. . . .
>
> Next Mr. Wickenden states that if a garden is mulched, light rains will do it little or no good because the moisture will be spread out in a thin film over the hay and will evaporate. Since he doesn't mulch, he must be speaking from theory only, which reminds me that according to all the known laws of physics, bumblebees can't fly, yet they keep right on at it.
>
> . . . Mr. Wickenden also declares that the ground needs the direct sun in the spring to warm it up, but I have found this to be true only in those sections where the earliest crops are to be planted. And since you have to pull the mulch aside anyway in order to plant, it isn't extra work to push it back ahead of time and let the sun reach the soil. Of course you have to be blessed with a mind which can figure that out. . . .[6]

Sorting It Out

If you are not entirely convinced by Ruth Stout's rebuttal, let me put in my two cent's worth. I'll try not to be so emotional.

First, to answer Mr. Wickenden's questions: Won't mulch prevent rain from getting to the soil? Yes, but not in the way he suggests. Coarse hay, which he chooses as an example, is one mulch that water penetrates easily. Water does seem to spread in a "thin film" on the fibers, but beads of water will collect rapidly and dribble through the mulch to the soil below. In fact, in this way the soil is moistened for a while *after* a light rain shower has stopped.

Matted leaves, dry-crusted peat moss, or *very* finely chopped hay spread too thickly *can* inhibit or even prevent any water penetration. Chopped leaves seem to allow more water through. Peat moss is less absorbent and less likely to crust if it is mixed with something else like pine needles or even with surface soil. The problem presented by any impervious artificial mulch is solved easily: poke some holes in it to let water through to the soil!

Shouldn't the soil get sunshine? I referred this question to microbiologist Dr. Doug Taff. He thought for a moment and said, "I don't see why. Look at a tropical rain forest. Roots and soil there *never* see sunlight."

Certainly, to germinate a seed needs sunshine for warmth, but it needn't be full strength. (I don't advocate planting most small *seeds* under heavy mulch anyway.) It is possible that sunlight on the soil could prevent some diseases from spreading, but at the same time it would reduce beneficial microbial activity. Don't forget: it is in the green leaves of plants where the action is. That is where photosynthesis, which requires sunlight, takes place—not in the roots (although important things happen there, too). Naturally, all green leaves should be kept above any mulch.

At what point do we decide that the soil is getting too much heat? Soil that is overheated can cause root damage. It is conceivable that soil might get too hot under black plastic in particularly warm climate—although proponents of black plastic mulch *insist* that the heat from the dark surface is given off to the atmosphere above the plastic, not to the ground beneath. It is my feeling that generally most worrying about the soil overheating under organic mulch is unwarranted. Organic matter is good insulation that discourages extremes in soil temperature.

Is it good for mulch and soil to be damp continuously? Yes. You might find it somewhat moldy under there, but all indications are that this does no damage to the soil or to the plants. Damping off is not a threat to healthy, well-established plants. If damping off *is* a problem in your area, do not mulch too closely around very young plants.

Problems and Solutions

By far, the vast majority of my own experiences directly contra-
dict the claims of Mr. Wickenden. Don't get me wrong. There are
some things to consider when deciding whether or not to mulch.
But I believe with every problem comes a solution. Let's look at
these one by one.

Can't Do It All

It's true mulches can't smother every weed. Robust perennial
weeds have been known to push up through straw, wood chips, and
black plastic. Heck, they've been known to emerge out of a concrete
sidewalk. I'm sure if I really wanted to prove a point, I could choke
out just about any weed, if I buried it under enough mulch. But it is
ten times easier just to pull the darned thing. Remember, mulching is
not meant to eliminate all your gardening chores. It simply makes
them easier.

Creates Nitrogen Deficiencies

Any fresh, light-colored, unweathered organic mulch will steal
nitrogen from your plants during the earliest stages of decomposition.
Wood-based products, such as sawdust or wood chips, are routinely
condemned for this reason, but hay or straw or leaves can also tie up
the nitrogen. Eventually, though, these will all add nutrients to the soil
as they decompose.

To deal with the temporary nitrogen shortage, you can supplement your gardens with additional nitrogen. Ruth Stout, you'll recall,
fertilized with cottonseed meal, which is rich in nitrogen. Or you can
try alfalfa meal (if you can afford it) or one of the chemical nitrogen
sources, like calcium nitrate or urea.

Inhibits Water Penetration

The knock against black plastic has always been its inability to let
rainwater through to the soil and, ultimately, to the roots. The same
can be said for some of the organic types, if they get matted down.
If you decide to use plastics, be sure the ground is moistened first.
Once down, make slits or holes in the vicinity of your plants to allow
for watering. You will be exposing those areas to weed growth so
you may have to pull a couple of stragglers now and then. Still, I'd
rather pull a handful of "volunteers" than weed out a whole bed.

Fire Hazard

Some mulches, like sawdust, are particularly susceptible to spontaneous combustion. A spark dropped into a peat moss mulch can cause a fire to smolder unnoticed for hours and be quite difficult to extinguish. Very dry hay and wheat straw can also catch fire easily. It seems pretty obvious to me that you need to be careful around these mulches. Don't smoke near them, and during extraordinarily dry periods water them occasionally.

Creates a Breeding Ground for Insects, Slugs, and Snails

I have to admit that when I look into the mulch in my own garden I feel like a giant parting the trees of some miniature rain forest. The decaying, rich-smelling organic mulches are alive with all sorts of creepy-crawling insect things, most of which I can't identify. Most of these guys aren't doing any harm. Their job is to break down the organic stuff so the plants can absorb the nutrients. I just leave them to their creeping and crawling and put the mulch back where it was.

You will find an increase in the slug and snail populations when you use mulches, particularly in years with a wet spring. These wet, slimy creatures love the dark, damp areas under a mulch, whether it's organic or black plastic. These fellows can have a field day feasting on your plants and definitely warrant a little attention. One suggestion is to pull back the mulch and sprinkle the slugs with salt. Or you can try one of the chemical slug controls on the market.

I have found a light dusting of wood ashes or diatomaceous earth on the ground at the base of my plants works well. The slugs and snails don't like to crawl over them because they are abrasive to their underbellies. Both will need to be reapplied regularly because they deteriorate with rainfall.

Blocks Air Exchange

Another knock on black plastic. I guess that's why the new landscape fabrics have become so popular. If organic mulches are applied too deeply or repeatedly, they too can restrict air movement. It's a good practice to get in there and stir things up occasionally. If you plan on supplementing your mulch because it has lost some of its color and appeal, be careful not to overdo it. Sometimes we add another 4 inches of mulch when we only need 1 inch to freshen the appearance.

Rodents Live in Mulch

Mice and other rodents drawn to the warmth and protection of a thick mulch may decide to take up residence there during the cold winter months. As food supplies dwindle, they may elect to start gnawing on your favorite fruit tree. To prevent this, never apply an organic mulch all the way up against the base of your trees or shrubs. Leave a space between the mulch and the plant. At least if the mice are going to feed on your tree, they'll have to come out in the cold to do it! To be really sure they don't damage your plant, you may want to put a wire shield around the base. Quarter-inch hardware cloth works quite well.

Ugly, Unpleasant, and Difficult to Handle

Here I must agree with Mr. Wickenden. Mulching *is* a matter of personal judgment. If you select the wrong mulch for your situation it can be a big headache. This is why I recommend becoming familiar with a wide range of possibilities. If your mulching repertoire is such that you can choose the right place for the right mulch at the right time, you can enhance the attractiveness and productivity of your garden while expending a minimum of effort, time, and money.

■ Chapter 4 ■

A Few Definitions

I find that good gardeners—probably because they like to *garden* more than they like to study about the technicalities of gardening—use gardening terms rather loosely. Ask ten gardeners to define a word like *mulch* or a word like *compost* and you will get the proverbial ten different answers. Interestingly enough, in the particular case of these two words (compost and mulch), you might find that the varying definitions not only are confused, but frequently overlap and are sometimes reversed.

Here seems as good a place as any to explain what we mean when we use some of the terms that already have been mentioned. These are not meant to be strict, inflexible definitions; in fact, you may disagree with them totally. They are offered simply as *working* definitions to describe what I mean when I use a particular word. Let's start with *compost.*

Compost is organic matter that is undergoing or has resulted from a heat-fermentation process. This heating, generated by intense bacterial activity, may develop temperatures as high as 150 or 160 degrees F. near the center of the compost pile. Heat is the distinguishing factor separating compost and mulch. In other words, if the material has not heated, it is not compost.

Sheet composting actually is more akin to mulching than it is to composting. It is an efficient way to build up the organic content in the soil rapidly. A layer of organic matter (leaves, for example) is laid on the top of the growing surface and then worked into the earth by a plow, a rototiller, or a spade. Once it is covered or partially covered with dirt, the organic matter decomposes very rapidly, but without heat. The end result of all composting is *humus.*

Humus is dark, rich, well-decomposed organic material. When the topsoil in a garden contains a generous amount of humus, the garden probably is a fertile, productive one. Rotting organic matter cannot be considered humus until you no longer can identify what the original compost material was. Humus can result from decomposing mulch as well as from compost.

Mulch can be any material applied to the surface of the soil to act as a barrier to retain moisture, to insulate and stabilize the soil, to protect plants, or to control weeds. A properly functioning mulch should have two basic properties: 1) It should be light and open enough to permit the passage of water and air, while at the same time 2) it should be heavy enough to inhibit or even to choke off the growth of weeds. Mulches can be divided into two fundamental categories:

1) Organic mulches might be defined as unfinished, unheated compost. These are probably the most desirable of the two for the noncommercial, home gardener. Any biodegradable material—anything that will rot—can be used as organic mulch. Vegetable matter is preferable to something like old cedar shingles, planks, or magazines and newspapers—although these *do* make effective mulches if you can stand to see them in your garden. The most common organic mulches are hay, straw, grass clippings, leaves and leaf mold, bark chips, and by-products like ground corncobs, spent hops from breweries, and buckwheat hulls.

2) Inorganic mulches, sometimes called inert or artificial mulches, are those that do not have plant material at their origin. These can be things that will never rot, such as black or clear plastics, or they can be mineral products, like crushed stone or gravel chips. There is also a something relatively new on the market called *geotextiles.* Geotextiles is the fancy word used to describe the landscape fabrics and mats being developed as mulches. These are spun-bonded or woven fabrics made from polypropylene or polyester. Maybe that's what happened to all those leisure suits left over from the 1970s—they were turned into mulch mats! Anyway, the geotextiles are kind of a compromise between black plastic and organic mulches, and we'll discuss their pluses and minuses a little later.

Here are a few other terms associated with mulching that are sometimes bandied about:

Seed-free mulches are just what their name implies: any organic mulch that has not yet or never will go to seed. This can include hay that has not yet blossomed. If you use a seed-free mulch, there is no danger of donating potential weeds to your garden.

Feeding mulches are those that will rapidly add plant food to your soil. Rotted leaves, manures, and compost (compost also *can* be used as mulch) are the most obvious kinds of feeding mulches.

Living mulches are flat, shallow-rooted, ever-spreading ground cover plants like myrtle, thyme, sweet woodruff, English ivy, and pachysandra. These mulch plants are generally associated with border flower beds, ornamental plantings, and rock gardens, but they can be both attractive and effective in the food-growing garden as well.

Green-growing mulches (or "green manures," as we sometimes call them) basically are cover crops like ryegrass or buckwheat, but they do meet all the definitions of a mulch. They afford fine winter and erosion protection. They can be tilled under and thus sheet composted, or they can be harvested and used for mulch in another part of the garden. Cover crops are used mostly in vegetable gardens or small fruit plantings.

Stubble mulching is a technique used more on large farms than in home gardening situations. The cover crop is harvested, but instead of burying the dead residue right away, the stubble is left in place to form a mulch that protects the land.

Cover crops like buckwheat afford fine winter and erosion protection. It can be tilled under and used as a "green manure."

Homemade mulches usually consist of materials that have been gleaned from household refuse. They might include dry coffee grounds or tea leaves and chopped paper. Vegetable refuse and garbage, if not tossed on the compost heap, can be thrown directly on the garden. If this somehow offends you, you can discreetly tuck it under mulch that is already there. Who's to know? Neighborhood dogs, incidentally, are not attracted to garbage that is buried under so much mulch that no scent can escape. Most of the homemade mulches are more popular with vegetable gardeners, but with the advent of chipper/shredders many are creating their own landscape mulches as well.

Contour mulching works much like contour plowing. If your garden happens to be on a hillside, try laying coarse mulch in topographically level strips. This will prevent your good topsoil from washing downhill. Your strips can be laid in the early spring, even before your earliest seeds are planted, or in the fall if you're planning renovations. If your garden is in a slightly "rolling" place, you may discover that your level strips of mulch create an attractive, curving, terraced effect.

Dust mulch is just dirt stirred up by a hoe or cultivator. The theory behind dust mulching is that digging up a layer of dust and spreading it over the garden will discourage shallow-rooted weeds and conserve moisture by breaking the capillary action cycle, which draws moisture upward from the subsoil. Unfortunately, all of this

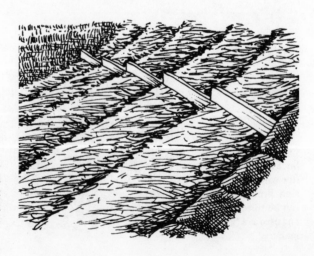

Contour mulching:
Terracing sidehills
and mulching in level
strips can prevent
your good topsoil
from washing down-
hill.

hoeing and cultivating means *more work*—which, after all, is what we're trying to reduce.

Fortunately for us, tests show no significant differences between soils under a dust mulch and those with an undisturbed surface. Usually the act of forming such a mulch kicks up soil particles and exposes them to even more air and more sun than if they had not been disturbed. About the only good this hard work accomplishes is that it *does* kill weeds, which rob the soil of moisture. Descriptions of how to grow certain crops, like celery, call for the plants to be "dust mulched." What they describe is closer to "hilling" than it is to mulching. If you like to *cultivate,* to introduce fresh oxygen to soil levels below the surface, go ahead and cultivate. But let's not confuse cultivating with mulching.

Permanent mulches are usually made up of nondisintegrating (not necessarily nonbiodegradable) materials. Permanent mulches like crushed stone, gravel, marble chips, and calcine clay particles are useful particularly in perennial beds, around trees and shrubs, and on soil that is not likely to be tilled or cultivated.

Another concept I'd like to explain is the distinction between winter mulches and summer mulches.

Winter mulches are used around woody plants as insulation. These are put down in late fall *after* the soil has cooled down. The idea is to keep the soil temperature from jumping up and down and heaving the plants out of the ground. Ordinarily, we are talking about

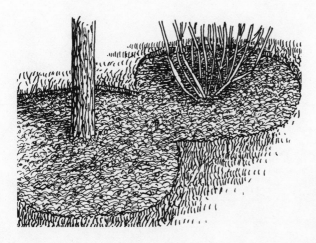

A permanent mulch of stone works well around trees and shrubs.

organic mulches when we refer to winter mulches, but the newer geotextiles may also provide adequate winter protection.

Summer mulches, or growing mulches, are applied in the spring *after* the soil starts to warm up. Their jobs are to warm up the soil, control weed growth, and retain soil moisture. These can be organic mulches, but most of the artificial mulches fall into this category.

I hope this chapter has helped clear up a few things so that the rest of the book will make sense. Please, refer back to it whenever necessary.

Types of Mulch

I hope that someday a psychologist will do a study on "The Garden as an Art Form" to find out how people expresss themselves horticulturally. How much does a person's garden reflect his or her own personality?

It is obvious that gardeners grow what they like and tend not to grow what they don't like. But what about the more profound things? Do sloppy-thinking literary types have poorly arranged gardens? Is a mathematician apt to have a neat, well-regimented plot? Do people with inferiority complexes grow tall sunflowers or cosmos to compensate for their feelings of inadequacy? Does it take a sophisticated, well-rounded, creative type to develop new gardening techniques and come up with new mulching materials? The mind boggles at the possibilities.

These are just some things to be thinking about while you're mulching or when you have nothing better to do. To be a little more serious, here is some information that I hope will influence *your* mulching personality—a rundown of the different types of mulches and how you can benefit from them.

Aluminum Foil

Aluminum foil is a relatively expensive artificial mulch. Unfortunately, it *looks* so artificial that many people find it unattractive. The only place I have ever seen aluminum foil used is in the vegetable garden, around warm-season plants. You can buy it in various widths. Normally a strip of foil is laid on the ground at planting time, and a parallel strip is laid 2 to 4 inches away from it. Plantings are

Strips of aluminum foil between rows serve as an insect repellent as well as a mulch.

made in rows between the strips. Aluminum foil is not a bad insulator, although most organic mulches are better.

Because it reflects the heat and brilliance of the sun—shooting light back up under the leaves of the plant, which helps to boost photosynthesis—aphids and other insects shy away from foil-mulched plants. Aluminum, of course, will never rot and it should be taken up in the fall. If a large amount of aluminum is left in the soil for a long time, there is some danger of aluminum toxicity. Foil crinkles easily and will break or tear if it is handled too frequently or if you walk on it. *Alumnized plastic,* polyethylene with a shiny metallic coating, is a little easier to manage than aluminum foil and has many of the same advantages. One strong point in favor of the foil over the plastic is that aluminum can be recycled.

Asphalt

Asphalt, which most of us call tar, sometimes is used by landscape contractors as a light spray to hold soil in place on steep banks while grass seed is germinating there. It disintegrates after about a year. Applying asphalt in this way is expensive and difficult because you have to rent or buy the right equipment and know how to use it properly. It generally is impractical for the home gardener.

Bark

Bark is probably the most common and versatile of the landscape mulches. It comes in all shapes, sizes, colors, and textures. It's available in 3-cubic-foot bags or in bulk. Bark chips are different from wood chips in that they don't include the heartwood of the tree. The bark is separated from the trees at paper mills and the like and then ground up into different grades and sizes. Bark decomposes rather slowly, but some of the commercially available shredded barks have been composted and may break down more quickly.

I have a friend who used to sell firewood here in the Northeast, and he spent big money on a machine that could debark his trees before cutting them up. When I asked him why he went to all the trouble, he said he made more money from the bark chips than he did from selling the firewood.

Redwood bark chips used to be found just on the West Coast but now can be purchased just about anywhere. Priced accordingly, of course (that means expensive). You can usually find them in several forms: as ground bark, as chips, or as nuggets. Redwood is a most attractive mulch in any of its various textures. It is not a particularly good source of humus, though, because it is extremely rot-resistant.

Douglas fir bark has many characteristics that make it similar to redwood bark. It is sold under the trade name Silvamulch. Tan bark, also available in some parts of the country, comes from white oak bark that has been used in the leather-tanning process.

Buckwheat Hulls

I have heard several gardeners call this "the ideal mulch." It handles easily, decomposes slowly, and does just about everything a mulch is supposed to do. It is inconspicuous, and can be raked up in the fall and saved for another season. Buckwheat hulls sometimes are sold under the commercial name Multex, and they are somewhat expensive. A 50-pound bag will cover 65 square feet at a 1-inch depth. It usually is applied in a layer that is 1 to 3 inches thick.

Dick Raymond, my gardening mentor, once remarked to me that using a buckwheat hull mulch just once is like introducing a mild hereditary mental disease into the family. Because the hulls contain an occasional seed or two, rare shoots of buckwheat keep cropping up generations later. But they never seem to amount to much, so this is nothing to worry about.

A buckwheat hull mulch does not retain soil moisture as well as do some other mulches. It also can be blown around a bit in a heavy wind and get splashed about in a real downpour. Because the hulls are dark, they absorb heat and can burn the leaves of succulent young plants that grow close to the ground.

Burlap

Burlap is effective for preventing erosion on steep slopes. It is widely used in grass-seeding operations, but it is hard to see how it would be of great value in the food-growing or flower garden.

For controlling weeds, it has to be rated somewhere near zero, because grass grows right through it. If you have lots of old burlap feed bags around, you might find use for them as a temporary mulch. But it seems like a waste of money to buy burlap strips.

If you plan to grow grass under burlap, leave it there to decompose once the grass has grown.

Cocoa Hulls

Because they are fairly dark in color, cocoa hulls absorb heat and warm the earth beneath them. They decompose slowly, adding lots of nitrogen, phosphorus, and potassium to the soil as they rot. For a while, at least, they give off a chocolate smell. A layer of 2 to 3 inches of this mulch is plenty around most plants.

Cocoa shells or hulls retain moisture for long periods of time and get slimy to walk on after about six months in the open. They may pack, too, and during periods of high humidity may develop molds on their surface. These are harmless, though unsightly, and can be put out of sight simply by turning the mulch. Another measure for preventing such visible mold is to improve the mulch's texture by mixing two parts shells to one part sawdust or pine needles.

Unless you happen to live somewhere near a chocolate-processing factory, you may have to forget it: cocoa hulls may be too expensive. Due to their expense, these may be best reserved for only the most visible flower beds and rose gardens. Donald Rakow, Ph.D. and landscape horticulturist at Cornell University, cautions homeowners on the use of cocoa hulls around some ornamentals. Their high potassium content may be toxic to some plants.

Coffee Grounds

Coffee grounds are a good homemade mulch, even though it may take a while to accumulate enough of them to do you any good (unless you drink an awful lot of coffee). Used grounds have a very fine consistency and will cake once they are put outside and are exposed to the elements. Use them lightly—never more than an inch deep—or else air may not be able to reach the plant roots.

I'd say coffee grounds are most appropriately spread in the vegetable garden or else sent to the compost pile. They aren't too flattering to ornamental plantings and might require some explanation if placed around the family's favorite tree.

Compost

Partially decomposed compost, of course, is a fantastic feeding mulch. After you put it on the garden it will disintegrate quickly and become humus. It adds many nutrients in the process. I have to regard the relative cost of a compost mulch as high. Good compost always is in great demand and the supplies almost always seem to be limited. If your compost-mulch is made up primarily of leaves, it may become matted if you ignore it for too long without turning it. Then water won't be able to pass through it from above.

Many municipalities now have yard-waste collection sites to help alleviate the landfill space crisis. You may be able to get your hands on large amounts of the "composted" material. Be careful with it. Many cities and towns are simply making big piles of leaves, grass clippings, and whatever else they collect, and don't have the equipment to turn and monitor the pile adequately. As a result, the material may not be decomposing properly and might have an extremely high pH. If you are concerned, take your share home and store it for a month or two in an inconspicuous place; turn the compost occasionally to give it some air. You may want to test pH to be safe. Once out in the garden and exposed to the elements, it should be fine.

Cork

Ground cork, as you might expect, is extremely light and easy to handle. It is *so* light, in fact, that you might also expect the first breeze would blow it across the countryside and that even a raindrop would dislodge it from place. Surprisingly enough, it stays in place very well once it has been soaked.

Dry or wet, ground cork is completely odorless. Its disintegration is so incredibly slow that it seems like an inert material, and its effect on the nitrogen content of the soil hardly can be measured. Like bark, it can be raked up, saved, and used from one season to the next. Cork has always been known for its insulating qualities, so it comes as no surprise that ground cork can be classified as excellent in this respect. Unfortunately, it is not easy to find unless you live near a large cork producer, and it might be expensive.

Corncobs and Cornstalks

Midwestern gardeners have known for a long time that ground corncobs and stalks make a fine and readily available mulching material. On the good side: ground cobs are an excellent weed inhibitor and do a good job of retaining soil moisture. On the bad side: its texture makes it somewhat reluctant to let rainwater *into* the soil. Cornstalk mulch won't win any prizes for attractiveness, but it might make a great conversation piece when the garden club comes to visit.

Ground corncobs may begin to generate some heat after a while. Keep the mulch away from the stems of tender young things. A 3- to 4-inch layer usually is enough. Don't grind up stalks that have been attacked by borers, disease, or worms; turn them under the soil. Or better yet, send them to the compost pile, where the heat will destroy most insects and diseases.

Cottonseed Hulls

Cottonseed hulls are plentiful and cheap, particularly if you live anywhere near a cotton gin in one of the Southern states. These hulls can be used most effectively around plants such as beans, which are suited to wide-row planting. (We plant bean and pea seeds four to six abreast in 10- to 12-inch-wide rows.) After the plants have grown 3 or 4 inches high, the mulch can be sifted down through the leaves, keeping weeds down in hard-to-reach places. Cottonseed hulls have a fertilizer value similar to, though not as rich as, cottonseed meal. Because they are so light, the hulls will blow around where there is lots of wind.

Cranberry Vines

Cranberry vines are sold commercially on Cape Cod, in Wisconsin, and in other places where cranberries are grown. The vines can be used whole (they are a little unwieldy this way) or chopped. They are good-looking either way. If you use cranberry vines for winter protection, you might want to hold them in place with evergreen boughs. They are wiry and light, they never pack down, and they decompose very slowly. This is why they can be used over and over again. Pea vines have similar characteristics.

Evergreen Boughs

Boughs probably are more attractive as Christmas decorations than as mulch, but they are valuable as winter protection, especially around newly planted or tender ornamentals. The Georgia Extension Service recommends them for erosion prevention, too. If you do use boughs to anchor the winter snow on your perennials, you will probably want to replace them with something else in the spring. They will have turned brown and ugly by then anyway.

Felt Paper

My experiments with roofing paper or tar paper were discouraging because the material was so difficult to hold in place without tearing. Builders' "felt" paper, which is not so brittle, can be laid with some success next to early tomato transplants. It will absorb heat and

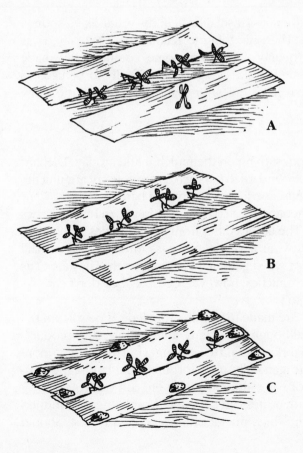

One way to lay "felt" paper mulch: Lay strips of paper next to the row to measure spacing, and cut notches for the plants with a knife or heavy shears (A). Slide the notched paper closer to the plants (B). Then slide the edge of the unnotched strip under the other. Make sure that all edges and corners are well weighted with stones or soil (C).

warm the soil around the roots. I wouldn't run out and buy roofing paper exclusively to use in the garden; it's expensive and not very practical. If you have some lying around the basement and want to use it up, do so with care. Some of the chemicals used in manufacturing are toxic to some plants.

Fiberglass

Fiberglass is completely fireproof. It also is quite costly and nonbiodegradable. It is pretty hard for me to imagine anything less attractive than strips of pink, aluminum-faced fiberglass building insulation lying in a lush green garden. If you ever have handled the stuff, particularly on a hot day, you can understand why carpenters always like to have their apprentices do the insulating in a new house. The itchiness caused by the fiberglass is enough to drive you up the nearest wall.

When it is wet, fiberglass insulation absorbs water like a sponge and then compacts. The only thing to recommend it, really, is its superior insulating quality. There are some commercially made fiberglass mats for sale that are designed specifically to be used as mulch. Some of them have holes for plants (and weeds) to grow through.

Geotextiles

These are the hottest thing on the mulch market today. Diehard mulchers are sitting around salad bars across the country arguing the pros and cons of landscape fabrics and weed barriers.

Some consider geotextiles a compromise between black plastics and organic mulch. The fabrics differ from black plastics in that they have spaces that allow air and water to pass through, and yet still block light needed for weed germination and growth. They aren't as beneficial as organic mulches, however, because they don't contribute anything to the soil.

Most geotextiles are made from polypropylene, a petroleum by-product polymer, although there are a few polyester products available. Polyester fabrics are said to last longer but they're also more expensive. These are generally used for lining big landscape construction sites and for soil stabilization and erosion control.

Polypropylene advocates can carry the debate one step further. They can argue over which manufacturing process is best. Should

One way to use landscape fabrics is to lay the fabric first, hold it in place with wire prongs, and put plants in place through slits cut in the fabric. The fabric is then covered with an organic mulch.

they be woven or nonwoven? Heat-bonded or chemically bonded? Needle-punched or glued? Who cares? We don't need to know all the details.

What we *do* need to know is how to use the stuff. Here there seems to be little argument. Basically, you clear the area of all weeds, lay down the fabric, then cover it with 1 to 3 inches of some other kind of mulch. Some manufacturers recommend planting first and then laying down the fabric. Others say to put the cloth down and make slits or X's where your plants are to go. I think you can decide based on your situation.

In order for the geotextiles to be effective, they must be covered or they will break down with exposure to the sun. Besides, they look better covered. Common covers include bark or wood chips, crushed stone, and cocoa hulls.

The problem is that weeds will still grow in the upper layer of mulch, particularly an organic one. These weeds must be pulled regularly to keep them from growing into the fabric and creating a new hole for other weeds to grow out of. It's also suggested that the cover mulch be turned occasionally to disturb any other aspiring seedlings.

As you can see, geotextiles are not completely maintenance-free and not too practical for annual or vegetable plantings. They could be useful for larger planting areas, walkways, patios, and places where plants won't be moved very often. They do provide you with one more weapon in the battle against weeds.

Grass Clippings

Almost anyone with a yard has grass clippings. Next to peat moss and hay, this probably is the most frequently mentioned vegetable mulch. Spring clippings can be used as a thinly spread mulch as your first vegetable seedlings come up. They will provide good nutrients, and the fine grass will not choke the tiny plants the way a thicker, coarser mulch might. It is better to dry grass clippings first. If they are spread too thickly they will make a hot, slimy mess. Not only that, they will smell bad.

If your lawn has a sizable population of noxious weeds, like dandelion, crabgrass, or plantain, or if any of the grass has gone to seed before you've mowed it, send the clippings to the compost pile. Remember, the idea is to eliminate weeds, not spread them around. If any herbicides have been applied within the last three weeks, put those clippings in the compost bin, too. It's just not worth the risk.

Otherwise, grass clippings are a good, cheap mulch, and they are already chopped for you if you use a rotary lawn mower. Some gardeners like to mix them with peat moss to slow down what would otherwise be a very rapid rate of decomposition.

Green Ground Covers

Appearance: excellent. Insulation value: only fair. These low-growing plants include things like thyme, violets, pachysandra, sweet woodruff, myrtle, and Johnny-jump-ups.

A few weeds will grow among these live green ground covers until the plants become firmly entrenched. Then the ground covers grow so thick that nothing else has a chance.

Pachysandra is pretty expensive and spreads very slowly, but once you have a patch growing well, removing six or eight plants to start a new patch is like taking a bucket of water out of a well—you will never notice they are gone. Try these. They are not a bad mulch, if you use them in places where you are not going to be doing a lot of walking.

Growing Green Mulches

These are often called green manures or cover crops. Buckwheat, annual ryegrass, and winter rye are all examples of conventional cover crops. Vegetable gardeners often spread these seeds after harvesting their crops to fill in the bare spots, keep out the weeds, and supplement their soils. Small fruit growers who plan well enough in advance may also use cover crops. The cover crop will remain in the garden over the winter and get tilled under the following spring.

Hay

Hay probably has been used longer than any other mulching material. And undoubtedly it always looked as unsightly as it does today. Chopped hay looks much better.

First-cut hay—First-cut hay normally has been allowed to go to seed. Many gardeners are reluctant to use it as mulch because it introduces a horde of weed and grass seeds into the garden. Ruth Stout, as you'll remember, argues long and hard that if the mulch is kept thick enough—as much as 8 to 10 inches—very few weeds will find their way through, regardless of the number of seeds in the mulch. Usually you don't have to *add* more hay. Lift what is already there, fluff it, and put it back down on top of the weeds.

Second- or third-cut hay—Second- or third-cut hay often is harvested before it has had a chance to go to seed. If you can get it, you might feel a little better about using this on your garden. All hay decomposes fairly rapidly and boosts the nitrogen content of the soil—although if it is quite fresh it will rob nitrogen for a short period of time when it is just starting to rot. Partially rotted hay makes better mulch than fresh hay for just this reason. Leave some fresh bales outside through the winter. In the spring they will be weathered and damp. Seedless hay is desirable for mulching raspberries, grapes, and young fruit trees. Make friends with a local farmer. He may be glad to get rid of any hay that has spoiled and is unfit to feed to his livestock. Have you noticed how much cut hay (some of it is weeds) there is along the sides of public roads in late summer? Rake it up! It's free for the taking.

Hops

Spent hops, nothing but a waste product as far as a brewery is concerned, is an inexpensive mulch wherever it is available. It decays very slowly and needs to be renewed only every three or four years if you apply it 4 inches thick and later rake it up and save it. You also might find that it has an objectionable odor at first. It is resistant to fire because it tends to stay damp, and this makes it an ideal mulch for conserving soil moisture. Spent hops can generate an overdose of heat to your very small plants, so keep it a little farther away from them.

There is one odd drawback to spent hops, and if you live in an urban area you might want to think twice about using it. It is very hard to keep in place because pigeons—believe it or not—find some food material in hops that is to their liking. They will pick it over continually and spread it all over your yard and lawn. This was such a problem in the Boston Botanical Gardens that they were forced to quit using hops as a mulch.

Leaves

It seems almost criminal to burn leaves or send them to the dump—they are nature's favorite mulching material. Leaves contain many of the essential trace mineral elements that the long, penetrating tree roots have retrieved from the deep subsoil. In addition to the basic nutrients that all plants need—nitrogen, phosphorus, and potassium—leaves also have such minerals as boron, cobalt, and magnesium in much smaller amounts.

Maple, birch, and elm leaves tend to mat and become soggy. If these are chopped, the water and air can penetrate them more easily and the danger of developing crown rot in some plants is lessened. Oak, beech, and sycamore leaves don't mat so badly, but they too are more satisfactory if chopped.

If raking leaves is a dreaded chore around your house, try bagging them up with your lawn mower. You can chop them up and carry them away in one easy step. There is no law that forbids mixing leaves with straw, ground corncobs, pine needles, or some other light material to improve the consistency of the mulch. Leaves in any state of decomposition make a splendid mulch.

Leaf Mold

What is the difference between leaves and leaf mold? Leaf mold has disintegrated to the point where the leaves are no longer distinguishable, and just the skeletal system of the leaf is left.

Rich leaf mold can be put to good use in feeding perennial plants that are difficult to cultivate, such as grapes, berries, and

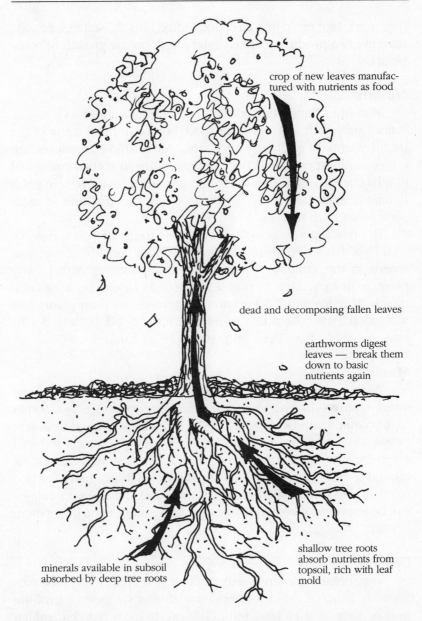

crop of new leaves manufac-
tured with nutrients as food

dead and decomposing fallen leaves

earthworms digest
leaves — break them
down to basic
nutrients again

minerals available in subsoil
absorbed by deep tree roots

shallow tree roots
absorb nutrients from
topsoil, rich with leaf
mold

The life cycle of a leaf. **Leaves, in any state of decomposition, make excellent mulch.
They contain many of the essential trace mineral elements that the long, penetrating tree
roots have retrieved from the subsoil. In addition to the basic nutrients that all plants
need — nitrogen, phosphorus, and potassium — leaves also have such minerals as
boron, cobalt, and magnesium.**

fruit trees. Leaf mold that has been mixed into the soil before seed planting can produce a spectacular effect on the growth of some plants.

Manure

Most of us think of manure more as a fertilizer than as a mulch. It does supply all *kinds* of plant food, but it can fulfill many of the requirements of a good mulch, too. Most animal manures are mixed with straw, sawdust, or some other absorptive material that has been used as bedding. Unfortunately, manure is in great demand, and what used to be free for the trucking is now sometimes hard to find.

The best manure is well rotted. Don't forget: If you use good, well-rotted manure as mulch, it will encourage the growth of weeds in the same way that it encourages the growth of any plant. You may have to pull a few weeds or use an additional mulch. Manure that has had no time to age can burn plants and will smell awful. Be a little careful with the dried, packaged varieties, too. They have been known to contain harmful salts.

Muck

Muck is black organic matter that has been retrieved from swampy areas. Its characteristics are similar to sludge — another highly fertile material — which is the product of sewage treatment plants. Muck sometimes is packaged in polyethylene bags and sold commercially. Once it dries it becomes a fine dust, which can blow around or be washed away by rain. Muck also disintegrates fast and needs to be replenished often. Both of these negative qualities can be improved if you mix muck with something else to give it more density.

Oak Leaves

Some organic gardeners make a point of keeping their oak leaves separate from others in order to use them as a pest-controlling mulch. John and Helen Philbrick write that an oak leaf mulch "produces an atmosphere which slugs and cutworms and June bug grubs and other very tender ones just cannot stand. Perhaps these tender-bodied creatures just feel puckery all over when surrounded by bitter leaves like oak."[7]

Oyster Shells

A lady named Ruth Bixler had trouble keeping anything growing in the shale soil of her Pennsylvania home. She says, "One Saturday I stopped at the feed store to get some food for our rabbit, and right in front of me I saw the answer—bags of ground oyster shells. I bought bag after bag and started shaking it over my soil. I really put it on thick and it was beautiful for the summer; not even a heavy shower disturbed it . . . The roses were never more beautiful and bloomed until the first snow . . . My Mimosa trees got through the severe winter without a single loss . . ."[8]

Exactly what aphrodisiac effect the oyster shells had on her Mimosas she does not say. Her success with them might be explained by the fact that oyster shells are "basic," or "alkaline." This means they have a high pH and operate like lime to neutralize acid soils. There seems to be no reason why this mulch would not work well on vegetables, too, especially in soils with a low pH.

Paper

Paper that is produced specifically to be used as mulch was first developed for pineapple plantations in Hawaii. It is treated to make it waterproof and is particularly valuable as a weed controller. I'm sorry to say that special farm equipment is needed to lay it neatly and efficiently over large areas, but the backyard gardener can manage it with a little patience.

Biodegradable black paper—This is kind of a nifty product. It comes in different widths and has a line of neat round holes cut down the center of the roll. These, naturally, are to accommodate plants. It seems to work in much the same way as black polyethylene and is certainly no more difficult to hold in place than plastic. It stays intact throughout the growing season, but it does *not* decompose on its own as readily as the manufacturer indicates it's supposed to. Once over lightly with a rototiller, though, and it pulverizes. It is not advertised as having any particular fertilizer value, and I have not seen any analysis to see exactly *what* it contains.

Newspaper, etc.—The home gardener can use shredded paper as mulch. Newspaper, for example, is an organic material, as are most paper products, and some inks provide trace elements essential to healthy plant life. Mulching with waste paper offers a great opportunity to recycle those stacks of newspaper that might be gathering dust in your basement. You might try shredding them with your lawn mower, too. True, paper that is shredded by machine is not particularly attractive, but it looks better than newspaper laid in folded sheets between rows of plants. It is also more pervious to water. Paper mulch can always be covered with a little soil to hide it and keep it from blowing. I know someone who uses newspaper to cover her entire garden, covers that with hay, then pokes holes through it with a ski pole to plant seeds. When everything is picked in the fall, she simply tills the whole works under.

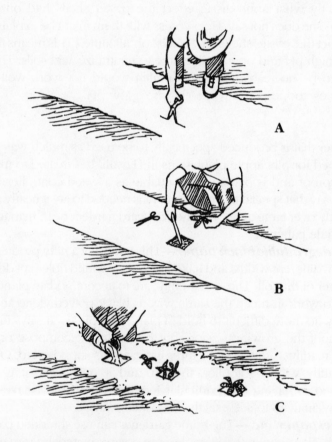

Commercial mulch paper in the home garden. **Lay the paper by hand and cut holes (A). Prepare the soil beneath the holes with some small tool (B). Add fertilizer mixed with water and make the transplant (C). Be sure that all the edges of the paper are well covered with soil.**

Paper Pulp

Waste paper, sawdust, and other trash can be converted into a mobile, flowing slurry by combining it with water and grinding it up. Years ago someone developed a machine called the Garbamat, which was like a gigantic garbage disposer, for just this purpose. The invention never was widely distributed, but the stuff it produced was found to be a very fertile mulch and was used as a side-dressing.

Paper pulp is used quite often in the hydroseeding process. That's the green stuff you see road crews and large landscapers spraying all over bare soil. It's a mixture of grass seed, paper pulp, nutrients, and water. It is particularly popular on sloping areas and in housing developments. The only reason it's green is so the landscaper can see where it has been applied. I also have seen some hot pink hydroseeding mixes used for wildflowers.

F. W. Shumacher of Sandwich, Massachusetts uses wastepaper products from the home and kitchen in deep holes he digs for trees and shrubs. He adds a layer of paper pulp, then a layer of soil, until the bottom portion of the hole is filled. The paper disintegrates, adding humus to the soil.

Peanut Hulls

Peanut hulls are available throughout much of the southern United States. Alone they make an attractive, coarse-looking mulch. Sometimes they are mixed with sawdust or pine needles. They weather quickly, decompose rapidly, and add good rich humus to the soil. They contain considerable amounts of nitrogen, phosphorus, and potassium. According to some studies, they make a very good mulch for tomato plants. There does not seem to be much to prevent our recommending peanut hulls as a mulch. Use them if they are available where you live. One possible drawback is that they might be attractive to rodents if not completely free of peanuts.

Peat Moss

Mention the word "mulch" to someone, and he is likely to reply automatically, "Oh yes, you mean peat moss." It's too bad that peat moss and mulching are synonymous in so many people's minds. Actually, peat moss has very few qualities to recommend it as a surface mulch—although there are lots of things to recommend it as a *soil conditioner*. Clean and easy to handle, it is a valuable

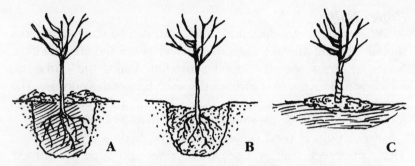

Use peat moss as a soil conditioner when you plant fruit trees. Set the tree in the ground at the same depth it was before transplanting. Use a stick for a depth guide if you need to (A). Fill the hole with a soupy mixture of new topsoil, peat moss, and water (B). Mulch immediately and protect the trunk against pests (C).

aid in deep-planting operations when it is mixed with surface soil and water. Trees and shrubs should do very well when they are planted in just this sort of soupy mixture. You should not have to prune the roots at all.

Peat moss is extremely slow to decompose. It is slightly acidic, but it does *not* sour your soil unless used continuously and in great quantities. It has practically zero value as an organic fertilizer, adding little or no nutrients to the soil. A 95-pound bale of pressed peat spread 1 inch thick will cover about 300 square feet. Soil under it should be thoroughly moist before peat moss is applied. Once it *is* in place it should be kept moist and loose or it may dry out and form an impervious crust. When it is loose, peat moss is astonishingly absorptive: it can soak up six to twelve *times* its weight in water! In other words, it takes an awfully heavy rainstorm to provide enough water to percolate through a peat moss mulch. To be blunt, find something better—and cheaper—to use as mulch.

Pine Needles

Pine needles should be available for the raking. They are light, clean, weed-free, and easy to handle. White pine trees have soft, flexible needles that make fine mulch. Needles from the red pine are coarser and may not rot for several years, but they are good for mulching larger plants. Cedar trees drop fine but wider "leaves," which make a great mulch for windy places. If you have ever tried sweeping them off a roof or walkway you know all about their affinity for staying put.

Pine needles absorb little or no moisture themselves, so water trickles through them easily. They can be used more than once because they decompose so slowly. Unfortunately, there seems to be very little worm activity under a pine needle mulch. Pine needles traditionally have been used around acid-loving plants, but they do not lower the soil pH so much that you should hesitate to use them on other plants as well.

Plastic (Polyethylene)

Polyethylene can be transparent, "aluminized," dark green, or black. Black plastic seems to be used more often than anything else. Because no light penetrates its opaque surface, *no* weeds can grow beneath it the way they might under clear plastic. It has long been applied as a layer under wood chips or stone to reduce maintenance and retain soil moisture.

Studies done at the University of New Hampshire show that its dark color absorbs the heat of the sun, causing the soil temperature to rise anywhere from 3 to 7 degrees F. on a sunny day.[9] Authorities at the University of Vermont, on the other hand, have argued on several occasions that the heat is given off to the atmosphere above the plastic because a layer of air—which inevitably winds up under the plastic unless you take special precautions to keep it out—acts as insulation. There have even been some studies done by the USDA on colored plastics and their ability to reflect light and possibly improve crop yields. Whatever the case, plastic of any color practically eliminates moisture evaporation. Water condenses on the underside and drips back into the soil. This also tends to keep the seedbed in a friable condition.

Since it prevents moisture evaporation, plastic also prevents water from penetrating. Nor does it allow the soil to breathe, which can lead to some serious disease problems in ornamental plantings. Tree and shrub roots may suffer from the lack of oxygen as well.

Black plastic seems more appropriate for vegetable gardens, where rows covered with plastic are alternated with bare ground. Most folks who use it lay the plastic before they plant, being sure the soil is fairly moist first. Be certain, if you try plastic mulching, that it is weighted down properly and that all the edges are covered with dirt so the wind can't get under it and blow it away. Cut round, **X-**

shaped, or T-shaped holes in the plastic film so plants can grow up and water can go down.

It used to be that polyethylenes were designed not to break down and you were left with the chore of pulling them up at the end of the growing season so you could plow. Well, several photodegradable and biodegradable plastic films are currently being tested by commercial vegetable growers. The notion is to tap into the convenience and heat and moisture retention of plastics while eliminating the hassle and expense of disposal. We'll have to keep our eyes peeled for a home gardener version down the road.

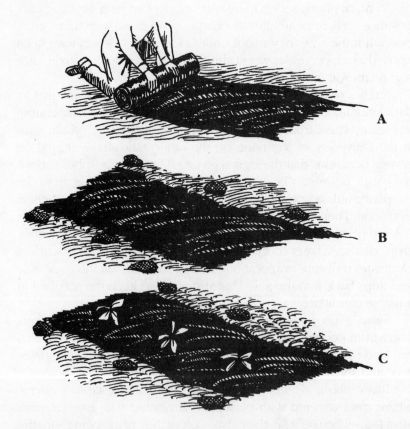

A

B

C

Black polyethylene mulch. Lay the plastic before you plant, being sure the soil is fairly moist first (A). Be certain that it is weighted down properly and that all edges are covered with dirt so the wind can't get under it and blow it away (B). Cut round, X-shaped or T-shaped holes in the film so plants can grow up and water can go down (C).

Poultry Litter

A local organic gardener of considerable renown, Jim Price, uses poultry litter with great success, though he chooses to refer to it by a different name, which courtesy does not allow me to mention here. But it is all the same stuff no matter what you call it. Frankly I was amazed at the size of his cabbages and onions grown with it.

Poultry litter might consist of straw, sawdust, shavings, crushed corncobs, plus the manure itself, but primarily it is the manure in this concoction that supplies nitrogen to the soil. The fact that it *is* a mixture is important. Straight manure might damage plants by giving them an overdose of nitrogen. Poultry litter still is available at low cost from many poultry farms.

Pyrophyllite

Pyrophyllite is calcine clay particles, which can be purchased in a fine-grained sand or in 1- to 1½-inch chunks. If you see bags of "Terra-Green Jumbos—Decorative Surface Mulch" in your local hardware or feed store, it is pyrophyllite. The pitch on the bag reads, ". . . Composed of 100% pure, inorganic, inert, non-flammable prophyllite absorbent. Controlled high temperature processing insures stability and sterility." Calcine clay should be considered a more or less permanent mulch, and it is about as decorative as adobe. If you really *like* adobe, consider buying some. Otherwise buy gravel: it's cheaper and won't absorb so much water.

Salt Hay

Salt hay or salt straw is light, clean, pest-free, and long-lasting. It can be used a second or third time. It never seems to get matted or soggy, and water penetrates it easily. It makes an exceptionally good winter mulch. A bale of salt hay will provide a light covering for an area of about 1,200 square feet. A 3- to 6-inch covering should be more than enough.

The problem is that salt hay is almost impossible to get. Most of it is made up of grasses harvested from salt marshes in coastal areas which, for plant conservation reasons, should be left alone. If you have some, you're lucky. If you don't, don't kill yourself trying to find it. There are plenty of other mulches to choose from that are cheaper and no threat to the environment.

Sawdust

Sawdust is frequently recommended as a mulch under blueberries, rhododendrons, and other acid-loving plants. Because it decomposes so slowly and seems to discourage earthworms, sawdust is not your best choice for a vegetable mulch. Water penetration through sawdust is only fair. In fact, some have complained that a sawdust mulch will actually draw moisture back up out of the soil. Another criticism is that sawdust will pack down pretty quickly, and it appears to be toxic and cause plants to turn yellow and suffer.

Sawdust is not toxic. It does, however, have a very high carbon content, mainly when it's fresh. You soil scientists out there know that a high carbon content ties up the nitrogen in a soil. The soil microorganisms become overly concerned with breaking down the sawdust and you end up with nitrogen-deficient plants.

Of course, all these obstacles can be dealt with. Unweathered pine sawdust does decompose very slowly, so just give it some time to weather and turn gray before you use it. Hardwood sawdust, by the way, rots much more rapidly than pine or spruce or cedar, especially if it is weathered. You can also combine sawdust with other mulching materials to improve water penetration and compaction problems. And simply turn over the mulch now and then to get air into it and break up the big chunks. No more than an inch or two of sawdust mulch is needed around most plants.

The nitrogen deficiency can be countered by adding extra nitrogen fertilizer to mulched areas. Calcium nitrate and ammonium nitrate are commonly recommended. Be careful not to overdo it: too much nitrogen can be harmful to plants, too. Nitrogen is highly soluble in water and any excess may leach away and end up in the groundwater.

Seaweed (Kelp)

There doesn't seem to be any way that seaweed can improve the cosmetics of your garden unless it is finely chopped. It *is* an excellent winter mulch and a great material for sheet composting. In most coastal areas it is free.

If the kelp you gather on the beach is *loaded* with salt, you might do well to rinse it off once or twice with your garden hose. But don't worry about getting it entirely salt-free. What salt is left probably will benefit rather than harm your soil. Seaweed donates potash, among other things, as it disintegrates. It also provides sodium, boron, iodine, and other trace elements.

Stone

Stone includes gravel, shale, crushed marble or limestone, even volcanic rocks and flagstones. It is one of the most decorative mulches, but it is highly impractical for the vegetable gardener. Use it where you are sure you will not till, such as around ornamental shrubbery and fruit trees. It is no longer cheap in most cases, but you can buy it in all sorts of textures and colors. As we have all seen, weeds find their way through crushed stone pretty easily unless the stone is underlaid with geotextiles or plastic.

Stone retains heat from the sun. It will warm the soil under it well into a cool evening. Stone obviously should be considered a permanent mulch. A few trace elements might leach out of a stone mulch over a period of years, but unless you use limestone, it probably is not going to dissolve noticeably in your lifetime. If you do use limestone chips, keep in mind these will raise soil pH and should not be spread around acid-loving plants.

Stone mulches clearly won't be blown around by the wind nor will they mat down in the rain or tie up soil nitrogen. About the only thing to be concerned with is picking up a stray stone with the lawn mower and sending it through the front window. For safety's sake, perhaps you could rake the grass near the flower bed occasionally and put the stone back where it belongs.

Conkilite is a trade name for lime or marble pebbles that come in small, medium, or large sizes. As advertised, this gives a formalized appearance when it is used as a mulch, but they recommend using 8 pounds per square *foot!*

Straw

Ideally, straw should be seed-free and chopped. A layer of chopped straw needs to be only about 1½ inches thick. Loose straw can be as much as 6 to 8 inches thick but is tough to handle and does not give a very tidy appearance. In either case, unless the straw is well weathered, add some high-nitrogen fertilizer to the soil first. Straw from timothy, oats, barley, wheat, and rye is widely available and relatively cheap. It can be used as a summer mulch around vegetables or as winter protection for trees, shrubs, and strawberries. It's frequently used by homeowners trying to start a new lawn.

A few things you should not forget about straw mulch: 1) it can be a fire hazard; 2) because of its high seed content, oat-straw mulches usually are pretty ineffectual as weed controllers—unless, of course, you are *trying* to grow more oats; and 3) straw is a common bedding material around the farm, so it's not unusual to find little creatures, like mice and voles, setting up camp in a deep straw mulch. If you do use it around your favorite plants, don't lay the straw right up against the base of the plant.

Sugarcane

Sugarcane residue, often called *bagasse,* consists of cane stalks that have been pressed, heated, and ground. Sometimes it is packaged and sold under the name Servall, and the cost is moderate. Sugarcane somehow never seems to weather or darken but retains its very light color, which some people find objectionable. Its pH is somewhere between 4.5 and 5.2, so it would not do a bit of harm to add a little lime to your soil if your plans include extensive use of bagasse mulch. Like peat moss, it is highly absorbent and will hold about three-and-one-half times its weight in water. Other than that, it makes a pretty satisfactory mulch. It will rot quickly because of the sugar content, so it needs frequent replenishment.

Vermiculite

Vermiculite (or perlite, which is similar) can be an excellent mulch — one that I heartily recommend for hothouse use. Outdoors it is not so good. This light, mica-like material is so light that it splashes around in a rainstorm. Nonetheless some gardeners claim they have used it successfully in very dry, very hot places outside. A layer of ½ inch to 1 inch is enough. Vermiculite is fairly costly and almost totally sterile, which means that it will contribute virtually nothing to the soil in the way of fertilizer.

Walnut Shells

Ground or whole walnut shells last a long time. Pecan and almond shells are very much the same. All are cinnamon brown in color and make a pleasing appearance. They don't wash away, they are fire resistant, and they are rot resistant. They absorb very little moisture themselves, so water percolation into the soil is good. An inch or two of walnut shells is plenty. Walnut and pecan shell mulches also might furnish some good minerals during their super- slow rotting process. Use them for several years.

Wood Chips

Wood chips from a brush chipper generally make excellent mulch. Regrettably, they are not a cheap item anymore. At the New York Botanical Gardens in the Bronx, wood chip mulch is stolen from beneath plants faster than the gardeners can put it there. That gives you an idea on how popular wood chips are.

As with sawdust and other wood products, the high carbon to nitrogen ratio of wood chips will temporarily tie up the nitrogen. There have been some other troubles associated with wood chips, but these are better ascribed to the people using them than to the material itself. Since wood chips lose their color and decorative appearance much more quickly than bark chips, some folks add a new layer every year. But most don't remove any of the old layer first and end up with 5 or 6 inches of mulch where they only wanted 2 or 3 inches. This overmulching can choke out shallow-rooted plants and promote canker growth on susceptible trees and shrubs. To avoid this, rejuvenate your chips every two or three years and add no more than you actually need to give them a fresh look.

Another problem that has been connected with wood and bark chips relates back to how the materials were stored. Landscapers and homeowners have found newly mulched plants, especially low-growing woody plants, suffering from leaf scorch, chlorosis, and defoliation. What happened? Chances are the mulch was "sour."

It's not uncommon for mulches to be stockpiled at the sawmill, garden center, or landscaper's for quite awhile before being sold or applied. Consequently, the mulch may turn "sour," or anaerobic. The lack of oxygen produces toxic substances like methanol, acetic acid, and ammonia, which can severely damage the plants around which it is spread. Packaged chips, if they are wet and have no ventilation holes, can also sour.

How can you tell if a mulch is bad? Mostly by the smell. If it's sour, it won't have that "cut wood" or "earthy" compost smell. It will stink like rotten eggs, ammonia, or vinegar. If your pile has soured, spread it out and let the air get into it. Turn the pile regularly and never cover it with plastic or anything that doesn't breathe.

Wood Shavings

Wood shavings are the thinly curled stuff you sweep off the floor next to a cabinetmaker's bench or the coarse material from a woodshop jointer or planing machine. It might also be the fluffy shredded wooden packing material sometimes called "excelsior."

Hardwood shavings are superior to the softwood shavings from pine, cedar, or spruce, which are notoriously voracious nitrogen thieves: the thinnest shavings are the worst offenders. They are somewhat less gluttonous if you mix them with cottonseed meal, alfalfa meal, or a high-nitrogen commercial fertilizer. We recommend chips over shavings if you like the idea of using a wood-based mulch.

My friend Ted Flanagan, agronomist and vegetable expert at the University of Vermont in Burlington, tells me that his father is probably the best mulching-material scrounger in all the world. "My

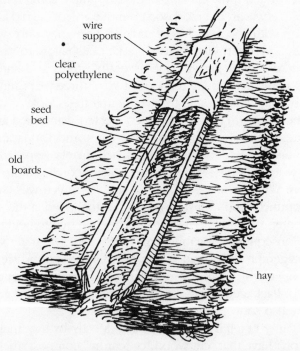

Try using organic and artificial mulches in combination. Some plants can be started outdoors well before the last killing frost by using this "poorman's cold frame." The boards catch the heat of the spring sun, the hay acts as insulation, and the plastic protects the seedlings from frost.

father will mulch with *anything!"* he says. But I can't help wondering if the elder Flanagan isn't second to his son in mulching inventiveness.

Ted has a marvelous collection of mulches, neatly displayed in shoe boxes with impressive engraved plastic labels on them. Actually, it is a valuable display in spite of the grief we give him about it, and he was kind enough to let me photograph the entire collection.

The collection includes rotting boards, old cedar shingles, paper bags, wrapping paper, paper towels, paper napkins, magazines, underlayment paper, corrogated cardboard (in rolls as well as in strips), shirt cardboards, stump chippings (which he distinguishes somehow from other wood chips), kitty litter, algae (from Lake Champlain, I think), dried silage (which seems to have distinct disadvantages), and a license plate (1968 Vermont registration #1045). Can you think of anything he's left out? What would a psychologist say of a garden mulched with Flanagan pop art?

How Do You Choose?

With a collection like Ted Flanagan's, how do you pick the right mulch for you? While there is no one perfect mulch, there are factors to make one mulch a better choice for a given situation. Specific mulches, as we saw in the previous chapter, have their particular advantages and disadvantages. How do you narrow the list? Here are some general guidelines to help you make the best choice.

Cost

Unless you are looking for something terribly exotic, mulch need not be expensive. There is no reason to mortgage the house or skimp on your plant selections in order to afford the mulch you've always dreamed of. Let's keep things in perspective. Mulching is important, but not *that* important. Shop around a little and price a few places before you decide.

Availability

The availability of a mulch often determines what the cost will be. The laws of supply and demand apply to everything, including mulch. What is plentiful and available is probably cheap—in some instances even free. Check with local municipalities, utility companies, and lumberyards. They may be dying to give away composted leaves or wood chips to someone willing to cart them away. Perhaps there is a processing plant nearby that has buckwheat hulls or peanut shells available. It might pay to check with one or two of the garden clubs in your area. They often have excellent sources for mulching materials (if you can get them to share them with you).

Ease of Application

In all fairness, if you plan to mulch on a large scale, we may be talking about a fair amount of work initially. On the other hand, we don't want you to be a slave to mulching. If you have an established bed, full of trees and shrubs, you probably won't want to slit dozens of holes in landscape fabric or black plastic to cover it. You might not want to hassle with the weight and bulk of crushed stone to mulch a small garden path. Pick a mulch you can handle without having to recruit all the kids from the neighborhood to help you haul it around.

Appearance

Speaking of the neighborhood, try to pick a mulch that won't cause people to whisper behind your back (unless you're into that). Experimentation is fine, but try not to offend anyone. Get a peek at what you're thinking of buying, then visualize how it is going to look in your garden. Will those bright red lava rocks go with the rest of the colors in your garden? Black plastic and straw are popular in vegetable gardens but may not look terribly attractive in the peony bed. This is a highly personal decision but definitely a worthwhile consideration.

Water Retention/Penetration

Certainly, you'll want the rainwater to soak down to your plant roots, but perhaps it's not as important when you're mulching a pathway. Assess your situation and choose accordingly. The same is true with air exchange. Plastics won't let air in or out, and this can suffocate plants; however, if your primary concern is weed control, maybe that's acceptable.

Lasting Qualities

In a vegetable garden, you usually turn the mulch into the ground at the end of the season. Chances are you'll want to pick a mulch that decomposes quickly. Conversely, mineral mulches, like gravel and crushed stone, will last for an incredibly long time, with a minimal amount of bother. Remember, fine or chopped mulches rot faster, while coarser mulches tend to hang around longer and demand less maintenance.

Staying Power

Obviously, you don't want to spend your Saturday afternoons chasing your mulch around the yard. If you live on a windy hill, lightweight mulches like straw or buckwheat hulls are unsatisfactory. Paper or plastic mulches will need to be anchored with pegs, stones, or something else. Small, fine bark chips can wash away with the first heavy rainfall on even the slightest incline.

Odor

Not a pleasant topic, I know, but it does need to be discussed. Manure and poultry litter do have their strong points and often smell is one of them. Sometimes the smell is more than strong—it's overwhelming! Grass clippings can also literally raise a stink. Some people even object to the smell of chocolate given off by cocoa hulls. Keep this in mind when selecting your mulch.

Chapter 6

Tips for Making the Most of Mulch

N ow that we know a bit about what to use as mulch, we need to learn how much, where, and when to mulch. I'll make specific recommendations for mulching vegetables, fruits, and ornamental plants a little later, but for now let's start with some general tips for getting the most out of your mulch.

- Don't try to stretch your mulch too far. It's like trying to paint with a dry brush. The end result isn't worth much. Try to figure out beforehand how much mulch you are going to need. For example: It takes 5 to 7 bushels of sawdust to mulch 1 inch deep on 100 square feet of garden space. In that case, as Ruth Stout suggests, you should get about twice that much. Almost invariably you will end up using more than you thought you would. You can always stockpile what you don't use right away.

- Always try to remember that bacteria and earthworms are strong allies for any gardener. Without help from lots of microbes in the ground, mulch would never decompose, and the vital elements that are tied up in organic matter would never be released. They pre-digest matter in the soil and liberate chemicals in their castings that plants can use for nourishment. They are also excellent indicators of how useful a material will be as a mulch. Dick Raymond often has said, "If the worms won't eat it, you should think twice about using it."

- Remember too that earthworms are affected by changes in season and temperature. They are least active during the hottest months and the coldest months. In the summer they can be coaxed into working harder if you keep enough mulch on the garden to keep the soil moist and cool. In the late fall, earthworms need to be protected from freezing. This is why we recommend mulching *annual* beds for winter before the ground is frozen hard.

- Be alert for signs of nitrogen deficiency when you use certain mulches. Some organic mulches, such as fresh sawdust, wood chips, ground corncobs, and some cereal straws, can cause a depletion of soil nitrogen. Because the bacteria that are breaking down the mulch and turning it into humus require such a large amount of nitrogen themselves, they take it from the nitrogen source most available to them: the soil. This, as I have already suggested, makes the plants look yellow and stunted, because they are not getting enough nitrogen themselves.

- If plants under a plastic mulch show signs of needing side-dressing, fertilizer can be dissolved in irrigation water run through a hose towards the T-shaped slits in the plastic. The stem of the T should point toward the direction the water is coming from.

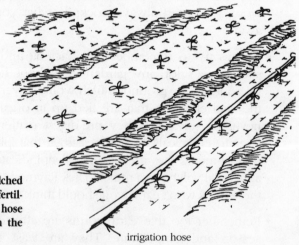

Side-dress plastic-mulched plants by dissolving fertilizer with an irrigation hose aimed at the slits in the plastic.

irrigation hose

A   B

Two ways to mulch row beds. In a rainy year, mound the mulch slightly to encourage some water to runoff into the area between rows (A). If it is very dry, make a shallow furrow in the mulch along the row of plants (B). The indentation will tend to collect water, which will seep through the mulch to the plants.

- In general, the thickness of your mulch is going to depend on the material you are using. Usually the finer the material, the thinner the layer will be. Mulch depth can vary from ½ inch for something like coffee grounds to 12 inches for something like coarse straw.

- Don't forget that plant *roots* need to breathe, too. Air is one of the vital elements in any good soil structure. Soil that is too compact has little or no air. One of the benefits of mulching, as you'll recall, is that it prevents this kind of soil compaction. But don't mulch so deeply that you undo this good by not allowing your soil to breathe through the mulch. Wet leaves that bond together and cake can also cause this problem. Fine mulches, unless they are applied sparingly, can compact and prevent air penetration, too.

- Normally you will want to apply thicker mulches to sandy, gravelly soils and thinner mulches to heavy clay soil. Avoid mulching at all in low-lying spots—places that are sometimes likely to be "drowned" with water. Although it may not always be necessary, you can remove mulch during a particularly rainy period, if you have time, to prevent the soil from becoming waterlogged.

- Another rule of thumb: Darker mulches like buckwheat hulls and walnut shells absorb heat and warm the soil beneath them. Lighter mulches, such as ground corncobs, reflect light and heat the soil less as a result. Choose mulch color according to

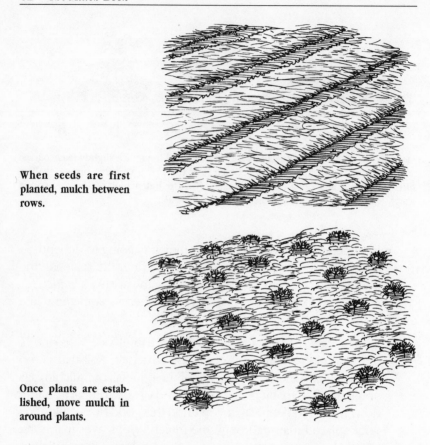

When seeds are first planted, mulch between rows.

Once plants are established, move mulch in around plants.

where you live and according to the heat-loving or hardiness characteristics of the plant you are mulching.

- Heavy mulch is most effective if applied after a rain shower when the ground is moist (but not soaked). If the ground is too dry to start with, it will tend to stay dry for the rest of the summer unless there is a real cloudburst.

- With most plants that are grown from small seeds, wait before applying your first mulch until after the plants are pretty well established. Mulch between the rows first, not right on top of where the seeds were planted. You can begin to mulch the seedlings just as soon as they are an inch or two higher than the thickness of the mulch you are going to use. Leave an unmulched area about 6 inches in diameter around each plant for about two weeks. Later, at a time when the mulch is good and dry, bring it right up to the stems.

- Do not apply wet mulches like spent hops or new grass clippings on very hot days, and be sure that they do not touch plant stems. When the temperature is above 90 degrees F., such mulches, being wet, tend to generate so much heat that they actually can kill plants with which they come in contact.

- When old mulch becomes decayed and compacted, replace it. Mulching promotes shallow root growth. Your plants can become like a spoiled child: because the soil stays relatively moist beneath mulch, roots do not have to grow deep and work hard, but can stay near the surface. This means that once you start mulching, you are committed to maintaining it. If you change your mind and decide to remove the mulch in midsummer, your plants may quickly die for lack of wetness.

- Fluff mulch with your hands or with a pitchfork once in a while so it doesn't get too packed down. If your mulch starts sprouting—because you have used oat straw or hay with lots of seeds or buckwheat hulls, which might contain an occasional seed or two—flip the mulch upside down on top of the unwanted seedlings to choke them off.

- If you recognize the advantages of plastic mulch but are offended by the sight of it in your garden, cheer up. Maybe you don't *have* to look at it. The plastic—or asphalt paper for that matter—can be buried under a thin layer of something else like pine needles, crushed stone, or hulls of some kind—even dirt! But I probably don't need to remind you that soil will wash right off any plastic that is laid on even a slight incline.

- Mold sometimes can develop in too-moist or shaded organic mulch material. You can get rid of it if you turn the mulch regularly. Mold does little harm. In fact, mold is evidence of a healthy decomposition process. It seems to offend the human eye more than it offends soil or plants.

- If you have bales of hay, try peeling off "books" or "flakes," (3- or 4-inch layers from the end of the bale) and placing rows of books between rows of vegetable plants. This will make a clean path for you to walk on during rainy days, as well as keep the weeds down. If any weeds come through in force, add more layers.

Books tend to be pretty dense because the hay is so tightly packed by the baling machine. Sometimes it is a good idea to loosen them by pulling the hay apart a little with your hands. This is an especially good idea if you are going to throw these books on top of onion sets or potatoes, which you want to grow up through the mulch.

- It is important first to cultivate around plants that are going to be mulched late. After-the-fact mulching cannot do much good if the ground already is dried and baked hard. This little bit of cultivating shouldn't make you feel too bad, knowing that you won't have to do any more there for the rest of the season once the mulch is in place.

- It is probably not advisable to use the same mulch on the vegetable garden year after year, just as it is not a good idea to plant the same crop in the same place year in and year out. A good mulching may last for several seasons. When finally it does decompose, it should be replaced by something else. Plants and soil seem to like variety the way you and I do.

- Mulches are excellent places for disease spores to overwinter and multiply. Remove and burn mulching material that you know has become disease-infested. Don't till it into the soil. In order not to multiply disease possibilities, the refuse of a plant being protected by mulch should not be used as its mulch. In other words, although chopped pea vines might be an excellent feeding mulch, use them somewhere other than on new pea plants.

Be a creative mulcher as well as a practical one. Experiment, read, and talk to your neighbors about it. Use your tiller and your chopper, if you have them—even your rotary lawn mower—to help you try out new materials and techniques that the "armchair experts" have not even thought of yet. It is *gardeners*—sometimes only moderately experienced ones who are not yet set in their methods—who learn most and can teach us much about gardening.

It is amazing to me how willingly and effectively gardeners exchange, modify, and implement new ideas. The body of gardening knowledge is growing so fast that it is very difficult to stay on top of it all. Please, don't be intimidated by the options and decisions you have in mulching. As I said earlier, there really are no right or wrong ways to mulch. Just good and not-so-good ways.

Here's How
with Vegetables

T he following is a list of annual and perennial vegetables with which I am reasonably familiar. Each item on the list is followed by a discussion of how and when these vegetables might need mulch.

While considering each of the suggestions made here, keep several things in mind: 1) the general mulching guidelines offered in the earlier chapters, 2) your own experience with a particular vegetable, 3) the climate in your part of the country, and 4) the idiosyncrasies of your garden, such as the soil condition, drainage, the amount of sunlight, and the likelihood of certain pests. As always, I will try to resist telling you what to do and will leave you the burden of deciding *if* and *how* and *when* to mulch *what* in your garden.

Just so this doesn't sound like a *total* cop-out, let me say I think you will find lots of useful information here that you can adapt to your own situation.

Asparagus

If you are just starting a new asparagus bed, mulching probably is not necessary at all until the second spring—although if you live in a cold place like Vermont or Minnesota, you will want to mulch for winter protection even in the first year. Hay, leaves, straw, old manure, and compost are just a few mulches that are excellent for winter protection of asparagus.

As you know, once a bed has established itself it will continue to produce asparagus for many years. In the spring, there is no need to remove winter mulch. The tips will come right up through the mulch whenever they are ready. Eight inches of hay mulch is not too much

Asparagus tips will come right up through the mulch whenever they are ready.

for asparagus. Its primary function is for weed control, but there may be other fringe benefits.

The people at Rodale Press make this suggestion: Try dividing your bed into two parts in the spring. Mulch half of the bed heavily with a fine material such as cocoa hulls, ground corncobs, chopped leaves, or leaf mold. Leave the other half unmulched until the shoots begin to break through the mulched half. Then mulch where you did not mulch before. Don't worry about weed control with the temporarily unmulched bed—those first asparagus shoots will poke through early in the season, long before any weeds take hold. If you are prompt with your second application of mulch, you'll still have excellent weed control. This technique should extend the asparagus season because the part of the bed that got its start without mulch will begin to bear one or two weeks earlier than the part that started out with mulch.

Beans

Dick Raymond says, "Beans generally take care of themselves." He seems to be right, but if you pin him down he will admit that they should be mulched in a dry year with something like chopped straw. This can be done about two or three weeks after planting.

Mulching is beneficial to beans especially because it inhibits weed growth. The finer the mulch the better, if you like to plant beans in wide rows. Bean roots grow close to the surface, and any deep or extensive cultivation to halt weeds will result in undesirable root pruning of the beans themselves.

Arthur Burrage, the famous New England gardener and writer from Ipswich, Massachusetts, says, "We found that the use of a thick mulch of about four inches of salt marsh straw or salt marsh hay is well worthwhile. It improves the quality, increases the yield, and completely eliminates the need for weeding—once the mulch is laid down."

I have had trouble growing lima beans. I seem to get a germination rate no better than about 40 percent, and the yield is low, too. If you have luck with them where you are, your lima beans can be mulched with about 3 inches of a light organic material as soon as they are 4 inches high.

I do plant lots of soybeans, in wide rows or just broadcast. Left to their own devices they do just fine, so I don't bother to mulch them, though I'm sure mulch would do no harm. Same with pole beans.

After planting some rows of beans in clear ground in my own garden one year, I poke-planted a wide row of green snap beans with my finger, through a walkway of hay books. I was a man of little faith, so the next day I went back to pull the books apart and loosen the hay a bit. The beans came up through the mulch just as quickly and, apparently, just as easily as those that had no mulch. They grew every bit as strong, if not stronger, than their unmulched counterparts. In fact, even in extraordinarily wet seasons they look greener and healthier. Possibly it is because, thanks to the mulch, fewer nutrients were leached out of the soil by the torrents of rain.

Beets

Beets like alkaline soil, so it is probably better not to mulch them with pine needles, oak and beech leaves, or peat moss exclusively. Use just about anything else. In fact, adding ground limestone or lime to the soil, or mixing it with the mulch, may be a good idea. Arthur Burrage says that "the use of mulch on the beet bed pays greater dividends than anywhere else on the garden." Ideally, leaves or leaf compost should be spread on beet plots at least once a year and worked into the soil as fertilizer.

A light mulch of grass clippings can be put down right after planting beet seeds, to conserve moisture and prevent the sun from baking the soil hard. As soon as the sprouts appear, pull this mulch back a bit for a while, as beets are highly susceptible to damping off. As the growing season progresses, increase the thickness of the mulch by adding more layers of straw or hay, and some time after the rows have been thinned tuck it in close to the maturing plants. This procedure seems to work well for turnips and rutabagas, too.

Beets respond badly to boron shortages in the soil. Chopped kelp (seaweed) is an excellent organic mulch that can correct this deficiency in a few weeks. Beets also thrive in humus-rich soil, and continuous mulching, of course, will contribute to this condition in your soil.

Broccoli

Broccoli can be mulched shortly after the plants have been moved out of the cold frame or greenhouse and set out in the garden. Any nonacid organic mulch is fine—it will preserve moisture and discourage some insects. Late in the season, because broccoli is naturally frost-resistant, the mulch can extend a plant's productive time. Broccoli can stand a maximum of 4 to 6 inches of organic mulch.

Polyethylene works well with broccoli. If you use it, lay the plastic, cut holes, and transplant through the openings. A little fertilizer and lime beforehand probably is in order.

Cabbage

After your transplants are well established, partially decomposed mulch can be tucked right up under the leaves around your cabbage plants. This may slow their growth somewhat, but they will grow tender, green, and succulent.

According to the Agricultural Experimental Station at the University of Connecticut, an aluminum foil mulch is especially suitable for cabbage. It discourages some disease-carrying aphids.

If you live in a warm climate—one that normally experiences mild winters—you might like to plant cabbage seed and cover the beds with a mulch sometime in the late fall—in November or early December. Re-cover the bed with coarser mulch, such as twigs or evergreen boughs, as soon as the seedlings appear. In spring, when you uncover them, you will have some hardy babies for early transplanting.[10]

Cantaloupes

Everyone seems to agree that cantaloupes and other melons need lots of moisture as well as heat, from the time they come up until they are fully grown. Advocates of plastic mulch feel they get an earlier and larger yield by using their black polyethylene film. This, they say, is especially helpful when the spring is cool and dry. The film helps to warm the soil, eliminates weeds, and maintains a more constant supply of water to the roots.

A thick organic mulch is designed to do pretty much the same thing. Hay, grass clippings, buckwheat hulls, cocoa shells, and newspapers work fine. It probably is better to stay away from sawdust and leaves. The mulch should be in place before the fruit develops, since handling may damage the tender melons. Once the fruit is formed, it will be resting on a clean carpet of mulch and won't be as prone to rot.

I like to see melon plants maintain contact with the soil because the runners themselves absorb moisture and nourishment from the ground. So I discourage the use of plastics or any organic mulch that the runners can not be tucked under easily. In fact, in a normal year I prefer no mulch at all at least until the fruit has started to form. Then, to keep the fruit clean, carefully set the melons on top of tin cans. This also makes them sweeter—I don't know why, exactly, but I think it might have something to do with the melons getting more uniform heat. A tin can mulch, you say? How could Ted Flanagan have missed that one?

Carrots

Mulch should be used very sparingly on carrots. When you sow them, you might want to spread a very thin mulch, say of grass clippings, over the beds to prevent the soil surface from forming a crust that the sprouting seeds can't break through. Water this mulch if you like, but be careful that the tiny seeds don't wash away. When the slender seedlings come up, be sure that the mulch does not interfere with them.

The Rodale Press offers an interesting suggestion for mulching carrots:

> If you are tired of the pesky brown worm that spoils your carrots, you might be able to foil it with a coffee break. Mix your package of carrot seed with one cup of fresh, unused coffee grounds. Plant the coffee with your seeds. It won't flavor the carrots as sprays and other poisonous substances do. Because coffee grounds are acid, they are good for plants that like that kind of treatment. Often it is best to mix ground limestone with the grounds before using it as a mulch or top dressing.[11]

Have you tried leaving your carrots in the ground during the early winter months to save storage space in the house? They can be kept there, covered with a heavy mulch of some kind to prevent freezing and thawing damage. Once dug up they won't keep long, but many people prefer them to the frozen or canned stuff you get at the supermarket.

Cauliflower

Cauliflower can be mulched in much the same way as broccoli. Mulch right to the lower leaves shortly after transplanting or lay plastic and plant through it.

Celery

The traditional way to "blanch" celery is with a dust mulch. Earth is pulled around the plants as they get higher, until finally, when the celery is full grown, the celery rows are about 18 inches high and only the green tops are showing. As a cleaner alternative, try an organic mulch rather than dirt to blanch your celery. Chopped leaves, which are less translucent than something like hay, are best. Whole leaves may dry out and blow away.

Celery that is protected with a deep mulch will produce crisp, tender hearts until Thanksgiving time or later. Ideally the heavily mulched rows should be covered with sheet metal, plastic, or some other waterproof material to form something like a tent. By protecting the ground this way, it stays dry and will not freeze too hard. There is no problem digging celery any time you want it, even in midwinter. You shovel away some snow, remove the tent, and uncover as much celery as you want to eat. Celery that is protected this way keeps better than in a root cellar.

Chard. See Spinach.

Corn

Some gardeners like Ruth Stout favor keeping a permanent organic mulch on their corn patches. At planting time they just run a straight line with a string and push their corn seeds down through the mulch with their fingers. After the harvest Mrs. Stout, at least, simply breaks the stalks over her foot and throws more hay over the old mulch.

Permanent mulchers argue that crows seem to be nonplussed by the heavy layer of mulch over corn. They normally will pull small corn plants nearly as fast as they show aboveground. If the corn has had a chance to get a good headstart under mulch, the plants will yield disappointing results to the average crow, who is after those tender sprouted kernels below the plants.

Here in Vermont, where I worry about soil warmth until as late as early June, I plant corn in the bottom of a furrow and use no mulch for a while. I cover the seed with about an inch of soil—which doesn't begin to fill the furrow—and stretch 12-inch chicken wire over the top of the furrow. The birds are unable or unwilling to reach the planted kernels or shoots through the wire. If you have no way to make a furrow (I just use the little furrower that attaches to the back of a rototiller), bend some 24-inch chicken wire down the middle to make an inverted **V** and form a tent over your row of corn. Be sure to close off the ends, or the birds will get in there and saunter nonchalantly down each row picking kernels of corn seed out of the ground as they go. Remove the tents once plants are 3 inches tall.

According to the old maxim, corn should be "knee high by the Fourth of July." At just about this point, when the corn is "tall enough to shade the ground," the corn is mulched. The stalks have been spaced or thinned carefully so they can be mulched without damage. The wire, of course, long since has been taken up. Use any mulch that will preserve moisture, and give the corn an extra boost by adding nutrients to the soil.

Cucumbers

Chopped leaves, leaf mold, straw, and old hay are good for mulching cucumbers. Mulch somehow seems to keep cucumber beetles away. It can be put around the plants when they are about 3 inches high and before the vines really start to extend. Cucumbers, of course, require much moisture, which the mulch will help to retain. Some organic mulches, as you already know, will invite some slugs, snails, diseases, and insects other than the cucumber beetle to your cukes. To be on the safe side, keep the mulch 3 or 4 inches away from the main plant.

Eggplant

Eggplant, especially if it is grown in the North, needs all the warmth it can get. Don't mulch it until after the ground really has had a chance to warm up. Also, the earth immediately around eggplant cannot be disturbed if it is to develop properly. Once the soil is warm enough, mulch will smother most weeds before they grow big enough to be pulled (which would disturb the eggplant roots, too).

The roots of these finicky plants prefer to grow and feed in the top 2 inches of soil. If there is too little moisture there, the leaves turn yellow, become spotted, and drop off; if it has too much, it will not bear fruit. Mulch can help to keep a uniform supply of moisture there.

Eggplant is also apt to attract flea beetles. Aluminum, laid temporarily on top of other mulch, has been known to foil these insects.

Garlic

Garlic can be mulched when the plants are 6 to 8 inches high. Use a fine mulch like hulls, grass clippings, or chopped leaves. See Onions.

Kale

Kale is an incredibly hardy vegetable. It can be grown nearly any time of year. A fall or winter crop may be left in the field, covered lightly with something like hay, pea or cranberry vines, or straw. Later in the winter remove the snow (one of the mulches kale seems to like best, by the way) and cut the leaves as you want them. Kale will sometimes keep this way all winter, if it doesn't get smothered by ice after a thaw.

Leeks

Leeks and scallions can be mulched lightly with anything from straw to wood shavings. Just be sure that the mulch does not interfere with the very young seedlings. See Onions.

Lettuce

Leaf lettuce does well in semi-shade and in humus-rich soil. A very coarse mulch such as twigs, rye straw, or even pine boughs can be used in the seedbed. As the leaves grow, move the mulch right up underneath them. This does four things: it holds the soil moisture, keeps the leaves from being splashed with mud, prevents rot, and maintains the cool root run that many plants—especially cool-season vegetables like this—require for optimum production.

You can apply as much as 3 inches of mulch whenever head lettuce is 3 or 4 inches high and has started to send out its leaves. According to Arthur Burrage, this helps to insure good plant growth. Every head should mature properly this way. Burrage says, "It has always been a pleasure to look at the lettuce bed. There are rows of perfect heads resting on a light brown carpet of delightful appearance."

Melons. See Cantaloupes or Watermelon.

Onions

Mulching helps onions. Almost everyone seems to agree on that. Even local folks who hesitate to mulch many things because they understand Vermont's fickle climate so well remark, "You can't kill an onion." They can and should be mulched during long hot spells. Chopped leaves can be sprinkled among the green shoots even if they are 2 or 3 inches high. Mulched onions should grow slowly and be more succulent than onions grown without it. A little more mulch can be added as the tops develop.

Ruth Stout says, "Onion sets may be just scattered around on last year's mulch, then covered with a few inches of loose hay; by this method you can 'plant' a pound of them in a few minutes, and you may do it, if you like, before the ground thaws."

Arthur Burrage uses a slightly modified approach. He puts down 2 to 4 inches of mulch whenever the onion tops are about 6 inches high. He says,

> For this mulch we use the remnants of what mulch was used in the bean, corn and pea area of the previous year. We find that the remnants are broken down into smaller pieces and are easier to handle in rows planted close together than something like fresh straw. The few weeds that grow are easily pulled and the beds stay neat looking all summer. Our experience has been that our troubles, at least as far as onions are concerned, are over for the season. Nothing is left to do except to pick them.

I have planted onion sets in three ways this year: 1) I planted them in bare ground and left them alone; 2) I planted them in bare ground and mulched them with finely chopped leaves when they were 4 to 6 inches high (this looks most attractive, incidentally); 3) I threw—did not plant—onion sets under about 6 inches of hay mulch. I've noticed that the growth of the onions in bare ground tends to be very slow. And it almost seems that those mulched with the chopped leaves stop growing entirely. But the ones under hay have done well, growing large bottoms. Explain that one to me if you can.

Parsley

In places where winter is not as harsh as in the North, parsley can be protected by mulch throughout the winter. It can be planted in cold frames in August—or even later—covered with hay, left in the frames all winter, and transplanted to the garden in the early spring. Parsley is susceptible to crown rot, so summer mulches should be kept 5 to 6 inches away from the plant.

Parsnips

Parsnips do not grow well in tight, compacted soil: instead of growing one straight root, they divide into three or four, which makes the root worthless. Mulching can help here by preventing compaction. But parsnips want a soil with a pH of about 6.5, so don't use an acid mulch. Like beets, they will suffer if there is a boron deficiency in your soil. Seaweed, again, has traces of boron and is often recommended for winter protection. Try some on your parsnips.

One winter I had the misfortune to be skiing on a *very* cold day in January. The temperature at the top of nearby Mt. Mansfield was about -30 degrees F. with a high wind. An abominable snowman helped me off the chairlift at the top of the otherwise abandoned mountain. When he spoke through his frosty whiskers, I recognized him as a friendly, lifelong resident of Stowe Village, six miles below. "Think this cold'll hurt the parsnips?" he asked. Parsnips do indeed have a cold-hardy reputation.

Most gardeners can eat parsnips from their gardens all winter if they are heaped high with leaves or some other protective mulch as

Parsnips will store well in winter under a heap of leaves or other protective mulch.

cold weather moves in. They store very well. Don't use them until after the first heavy frost; they won't have reached their peak of quality until then anyway. Most folks think they are best in November and December. Will they survive -30 degrees F.? I keep forgetting to ask my mountaintop friend how his fared.

Peas

It is easy to overdo mulching peas in a cool climate like ours. The soil around peas *does* need to be cool and damp. In dry soil they will not germinate well and a large percentage of the seeds will be lost. In late spring around here, we usually don't have any trouble meeting either of these conditions without using mulch.

Peas will grow through a light straw mulch. As the plants get started, increase the mulch to insulate the soil from the heat of the sun. This way you are almost assured of a cool, moist root run.

To grow peas in much warmer places, or to grow pea varieties like Wando later in the summer, mulch with a thin layer of grass clippings, straw, or hay when the seeds are sown. (We broadcast peas in some places and then bury them just under the surface with the rototiller.) As the plants get started, you can increase the mulch to insulate the soil from the atmosphere and the hot sun. This way you can almost assure yourself of a cool, moist root run.

One June, just as I was finishing planting my own peas in the traditional way (in rows without mulch), my wife called me to lunch. I still had a large fistful of seeds in my hand. Indolent fellow that I am (also very hungry at that point, and a *little* curious, too, if the truth be known), I more or less threw the seeds away instead of putting them carefully back in the bag. In what was a furtive sweeping gesture I quickly tossed the evidence of my own wastefulness under the rug of very heavy hay mulch. To my surprise, even though they actually were never planted in the soil, they came up en masse and looked healthy and green.

We broadcast the same variety (Little Marvel) in a rather shady section of one of our gardens, tilled them under, and covered them with some winter rye that we had just cut from another section of the garden. The results *there* were very disappointing. So few plants came up that my wife's comment was that "they weren't even neighbors!" What the problem was, we are not sure.

The last time you pick your peas each season, pull up the whole vine before you remove the pods. This should help save your back. The vines should be stacked and saved, too. Chopped or whole, they are a nitrogen-rich mulch that can be used anywhere on the garden, except on other peas.

Peppers

The growing habits of sweet peppers are very much like those of tomatoes. We often plant these two at the same time as companion plants. Early plants respond well to a black-paper mulch. This will collect the heat of the day and help maintain a warm soil temperature for a while into the night. Later the paper mulch can be taken off and replaced with an organic mulch, or not replaced at all.

I have learned that pepper plants grown under hay mulch may be stunted and slow to mature. On the other hand, my own pepper plants, which are surrounded with dark, chopped leaf mold mixed with alfalfa meal, are quite a bit ahead of some of the peppers in other gardens. Peppers and dark-colored mulches seem to go well together.

Potatoes

Potatoes, if you use mulch, don't even need to be planted! As Ruth Stout says, "Many people have discovered that they can lay seed potatoes on last year's mulch, or on the ground or even on sod, cover them with about a foot of loose hay, and later simply pull back the mulch and pick up the new potatoes."[12]

This oversimplification may be what some would consider another unfortunate Stoutism, but you *can* grow potatoes "under mulch, in mulch, on top of mulch—almost any way in fact—and get satisfactory results." You can harvest early potatoes from their thick mulch bed and then replace the covering.

Deep mulch also seems to thwart the potato bug, whose larva winters in the soil. Apparently these fellows are reluctant to climb up the potato stem through the thick hay.

Pumpkins

Pumpkins will profit from freshly cut hay, composted leaves, straw, and cow manure. Mulch around each hill. Any coarse mulch that keeps the fruit off the ground can be used as the crop starts to mature.

Radishes

Mulch is not recommended for quick-growing plants like radishes. Normally there is not enough time for the mulch to do them any good. For the most part, plants that prefer cool, moist soil respond better to mulches than those that revel in hot sun and dry soil.

Rhubarb

Again, I like this description from the Rodale book: Thick stalks of rhubarb result from continuous heavy feeding. To keep the soil up to the standard necessary, spread a thick mulch of strawy manure over the bed after the ground freezes in the winter. In the spring, rake the residue aside to allow the ground to warm and the plants to sprout. Then draw the residue, together with a thick new blanket of straw mulch up around the plants. Hay, leaves, or sawdust also make excellent mulches for rhubarb.

Rutabaga. See Beets.

Spinach

Mulching spinach and similar vegetables such as Swiss chard seems like a waste of time to me since it's such a short-season crop, but some say that it can be mulched with grass clippings, chopped hay, or ground corncobs and be better for it. Since spinach does not do well in acid soil, avoid peat moss, oak and beech leaves, pine needles, and sawdust. In any case, I don't advise putting down a summer mulch until after the leaves have had a chance to make a good growth.

Squash

Squash can use an extra-special dose of mulch, especially during hot, dry spells. The mulch, whether it be rotted sawdust, compost, hay, or just leaves, can be as deep as 4 inches. Leave the center open so that some heat can get to the middle of the plant. The mulch over the rest of the patch will preserve moisture and discourage some bugs. I probably don't need to remind you about how much space is taken up by squash. Be sure that you have plenty of mulch before you commit yourself. Don't bother mulching winter squash.

Kerr Sparks, a friend of mine, grows beautiful zucchini and acorn squash in a rock mulch—and I mean *rocks,* not crushed stone. Some of the rocks are 10 to 12 inches in diameter. His wife and some of his neighbors started worrying about his sanity when he started packing these big stones around his young squash plants. "They didn't do much at first," he says, "but later in the spring when the sun got to the rocks, it was frightening. The plants grew as much as 7 inches in a day!"

He gave me one huge zucchini to try. It was every bit as tender as the young, small zucchini I normally prefer. And the seeds, for some reason, were small, few, and far between. This must have something to do with the fast growth the squash makes as it rests on the warm stones. Do you have a lot of rocks around your place you don't know what to do with?

Sweet Potatoes

Sweet potatoes are ravenous feeders and are happiest in plenty of moisture. Compost is an ideal mulch for just these reasons. Old leaves and grass clippings make a good organic side-dressing, as do the old standbys, hay and straw. If you plant sweet potatoes in hills, mulch them well, fertilize them well, and allow lots of room for them to develop.

Tomatoes

Some vegetables such as tomatoes (as well as peppers and corn) need thoroughly warmed soil to encourage ideal growth. A mulch that is applied too early in the spring, before soil temperatures have had a chance to climb a little in frost zone areas, will slow such crops. Generally, in colder climates like ours, tomatoes need less mulch. Dark-colored mulches can help seal in heat and moisture.

A good time to mulch is right after the flowers appear. Blossom-end rot can be caused by a variable moisture supply. Mulch keeps a more consistent supply of moisture around the roots of the plants. I have used many different things: chopped alfalfa hay, chopped pea vines, chopped leaves and straw. Early plantings have been mulched with felt paper to keep the soil warm. If you find that you have lots of mulch and few sticks to use as tomato stakes, forget about staking. Let your plants run around freely over the mulch and let the fruit ripen there.

Turnips. See Beets.

Watermelon

Here is still another plant that should not be mulched until the soil is really warm. How many gallons of water do you suppose there are in one large watermelon? Obviously they demand all kinds of soil moisture. The best time to apply mulch is when the soil has been dampened thoroughly. Up to 6 inches of mulch can be spread over the entire patch, if you like, to prevent rot and to keep the fruit dirt-free.

▬ Chapter 8 ▬

Here's How with Fruits

I wish that this chapter could have a title like "Mulching Fruits: a Month-by-Month Calendar." Unfortunately, seasons and climates vary so much throughout the country that such an approach would be inaccurate and confusing to many people. We will have to be content with general descriptions of what to do in spring, summer, autumn, and winter.

Spring
As the snow starts to melt during those first warm, sunny days of spring, gardeners everywhere start champing at the bit. This is the season for restraint. Because most fruits are perennial plants already in place, it is easy to get excited on a day with 60-degree temperatures and jump the gun. Think about other things if you can. Try to remind yourself that there aren't many things to worry about in the garden itself just yet. Loosen mulch where it has been crushed by snow, if you like, but don't remove it too early. Spring is a good time to scout around and see what you can scavenge in the way of mulching materials.

Early spring is the time to plow, spade, or rototill winter mulch into seedbeds where you will be planting your annual plants. Don't remulch perennial fruits until at least two weeks after the average date of the last killing frost, whenever that may be where you live. Give the earth plenty of time to warm up.

By mid-April here in Vermont we are just *beginning* to remove winter mulch from the perennials. This is about three or four weeks after the snow has left our valleys. This date probably will be earlier where you are. Remember: Removing too much mulch from perennial plants too early does *not* help the soil and the roots to warm up.

It may warm it for a few hours, but after the next hard freeze and subsequent thaw (and we have plenty of those in late April and May) plants may be frost-heaved right out of the ground and die of root exposure.

Move protective mulch away from plants gradually and let it lie off to the side, but within easy reach. Take off one thin layer at a time, waiting several days before you remove the next layer. This painfully slow process gives your plants a chance to harden. Josephine Nuese says, "Don't whip off winter protection until the soil beneath the plant has thawed out. Strong March winds and strong March sun, both dehydrating, can drain the essential moisture which the still frozen roots can't replace. Don't be misled by shallow surface thawing. If you poke down with a stick and can feel ice, leave the mulch."[13]

As much as anything else, mulch should be kept on so the roots and tender shoots won't grow too *soon* and get nipped by frost. If it's possible, remove the final layer of mulch on a cloudy day so that any young shoots that *have* started are not blasted suddenly by brilliant sunshine. Once the winter mulch is off completely, leave it off for several days, or even a couple of weeks, before you start to mulch again.

In the *late* spring start mulching again, to conserve moisture and control weeds before they get a head start. This is a good time to fertilize around fruit trees and berry bushes by adding some sort of feeding mulch, which will contribute humus and nourish the plants. Nitrogen-rich grass clippings usually abound at this time. Use them, but dry them first. Mulch far enough away from your fruit trees—out at least to the "drip line" (that's the outer perimeter of the tree if you are looking straight down on it)—so you can be sure your mulch is doing some good directly over the tiny feeder roots.

Summer

Summer is the time when mulching should start to pay dividends. During hot spells, roots should thrive in the weedless, cool, moist ground under mulch. You do nothing now except have a look every now and again and renew the mulch wherever weeds show signs of getting the upper hand. Pull any persistent weeds that keep showing up.

Be crafty about choosing materials for summer mulching. Because your fruits will not be tilled, encouraging earthworms into your perennial beds becomes particularly important in order for your soil to get some aeration. Avoid using mulches like sawdust, pine needles, and redwood by-products because earthworms avoid them. A continuous mulch around thick-stemmed shrubs and trees should be a coarse, heavy material that allows plenty of water through, but that is not going to decay too rapidly (it should last for several years). Top-dress through the mulch with fertilizer whenever it seems appropriate.

One thing to look out for: There is danger of crown rot in small fruits—strawberries, for example—during the early summer months. If there have been especially heavy rains, postpone your mulching until the soil no longer is waterlogged. Do not allow mulches like peat moss, manure, compost, spent hops, or ground corncobs to touch the bases of your plants. Leave mulch-free circles around the stems several inches in diameter. The idea here is to permit the soil to stay dry and open to the air around the immediate area of the plant. Most other mulches do not present this problem.

Mulch should be maintained in a young or dwarf fruit orchard throughout the summer. An organic gardener and farmer named Chuck Pendergast reports:

> In early fruit orcharding, the practice was to let the trees go to grass. In other words, the land surrounding the trees in an orchard was not cultivated and plant life was allowed to establish itself there. Year after year, this resulted in a gradual building-up of the sod. The more time it has, the tighter sod will become. Eventually there was a conflict between the grasses covering the ground around the trees and the trees which were being deprived of necessary quantities of water. Hence the practice of keeping the land in an orchard free from growth began.
>
> The immediate results of this practice were favorable. The trees' health and yield improved . . . As it is hard to prevent cover grasses from becoming detrimental once they become established, mulching is now a widespread practice in orcharding . . . We've learned something and put it to wise use.[14]

Autumn

The longer the perennial's roots can stay at work in the fall the better—up to a point. Late mulching can prolong a plant's growing season because it provides a buffer zone against frost. Roots will

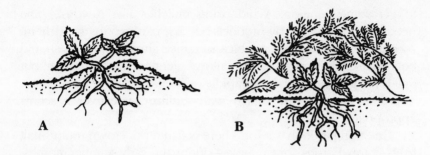

Alternate freezing and thawing can heave plants out of the ground, causing root damage (A). Evergreen boughs anchor snow and offer fine winter protection for perennial plants (B).

continue to grow in soil as long as there is still moisture available there. When the soil water freezes and is unavailable to roots, they stop. Increase your mulch volume gradually for a while to insulate the soil and to prevent early freezing of soil moisture.

Once the frost has been on the pumpkin more than a couple of times, your plants probably should be given a hardening-off period similar to the one you gave them in the spring. Remove the mulch gradually until the plants are obviously dormant and the ground is frozen.

By now you should be collecting materials for winter mulching. Maybe you will want to cut evergreen boughs. They do a great job of holding snow (a superb mulch itself) in places where it might otherwise be blown away. After harvest time, push mulch back away from fruit trees, leaving an open space around the trunks. If you anticipate a winter rodent problem in berry bushes, grapes, or dwarf fruit trees if mulched with seedy materials, don't forget that you can wrap wire mesh, hardware cloth, or plastic protectors around trunks and berry canes. If you are really concerned, or if you're feeling particularly vindictive because of previous experience with rodents, you can always throw a little poison grain into the mulch. That should slow them down. Avoid this, though, if you have pets or small children who might come in contact with the mulch.

Fall is the best time to make use of your chopper by grinding up plant residues for future use as mulch. Use your rototiller, if you have one, for sheet-composting leaves between rows. Till in the summer mulch, too.

Winter

Should winter mulching of perennials be done before or after the ground is frozen? This has been a source of much controversy and confusion in mulching circles. Don't *you* be confused: remember, this chapter has to do with perennial fruits. Mulch your *annual* beds early—before frost really has settled into the soil—so that earthworms and beneficial microorganisms can stay at work longer during the cold months.

Some argue that a garden should be left naked and exposed for the winter, and John and Helen Philbrick have written, "Mulch should not be left on over the winter because it prevents the beneficial action of the frost in the earth. Moisture should not be hindered from "coming and going" during the seasons of snow and ice. If protective mulch is in such a condition that it will break down during the winter and become part of the topsoil, it may be left. But the home gardener should study this subject carefully and be sure he knows exactly what he is doing and why he is doing it."[15]

I *have* made a study of this—a cursory one, at least. I asked the question, "Why does Mother Nature arrange to have her trees drop their leaves, and then later see to it that a heavy blanket of snow insulates the ground even more? Is winter mulching then a bad thing?" We can conclude that your garden, *particularly* your perennials, *should* have winter mulch. But there is no hurry to put it there.

Vermonters laugh unsympathetically at "down-country" people who bundle up under many layers of winter clothing in a futile effort to keep cold out and keep themselves warm. They learned generations ago to dress to keep their own body warmth *in*.

Winter mulch acts in the same way, except that it keeps winter soil *frozen*—even during thaws. Winter moisture and frost ought to be allowed to penetrate the soil before you lay down a heavy winter mulch. Then, if the mulch keeps the frost in, the plants cannot be "heaved" out of the ground when the soil expands and contracts on alternately freezing and thawing days.

Winter mulch protects perennial foliage from drying winds and too-bright winter sunshine. It prevents the absorption of heat in the spring and doesn't allow a thing to grow until after the last killing frost, when finally it is removed. The initial question (in case you've forgotten): Should winter mulching of perennials be done before or after the ground is frozen? The answer: after.

Last question: How much winter mulch is enough? I suppose that it is possible to smother plants under too much winter mulch. One approach to the problem might be to find out from your local bureau of the United States Weather Service the average frost depth in your area. Then roughly estimate how deep your plants' roots are. Once you know this, you might find that Dr. D. E. Pfeiffer provides a clue. He says, "Winter mulch does the same thing that snow does: it insulates the soil to the same depth as the height of the mulch. If there is a three foot snowfall, the effect of the snow reaches down to a depth of three feet. A mulch acts in the same way . . ."[16] This doesn't mean that you have to mulch to a level equivalent to the bottom of the frost level. That would mean as much as 4 feet of mulch in Vermont! It only means that you should mulch to a height that is a little greater than your perennial plants' roots are deep—that is, if the frost level where you live goes below that point.

Here are some suggestions for mulching some of the most commonly raised backyard fruits.

Fruit Trees

I am going to cheat a little here and lump all the tree fruits together. I couldn't find anything to justify treating peaches differently from pears, or cherries differently from apples. I did find mulching to be highly recommended for fruit trees. As with other plants, mulching will help regulate soil moisture and soil temperature, control weeds, and improve the soil structure. An additional benefit to mulching around your fruit trees is that a nice, soft bed of straw or leaf mulch will cushion fruits that drop from the tree. If you are delinquent in harvesting your apples, perhaps you won't have to make so much applesauce.

One real danger when mulching fruit trees is the threat of rodent damage. These animals have a particular taste for fruit trees and, as I said earlier, mulched trees are even more enticing. Be sure to leave a space of several inches between your mulch and the base of the tree and use a tree guard.

Straw, hay, grass clippings, and sawdust are excellent choices for fruit trees. These break down relatively fast and have to be replenished. Woody mulches or coarsely ground corncobs, which will last anywhere from three to five years, may involve less work. If you decide to use these longer-lasting mulches, don't forget that your

You may want to lay some soft mulch under the branches of your fruit trees as harvest time gets closer. It will keep your "drops" from being bruised.

trees still should be fertilized once a year or so. Black plastic can also be spread around the base of the trees in the spring to control weeds, but pick it up before late fall to eliminate potential nesting sites for mice.

Organic mulches can be applied to a depth of 6 inches. It will decompose to about half that thickness and you may have to add more. The mulch should be kept at or near that 6-inch depth for good weed control. If you can stand the look of it, apply the mulch out from the tree trunk to slightly beyond the spread of the branches. This gives those falling fruits a larger target and protects more of the root area.

Strawberries

W. H. Thies says that organic mulching can make the difference between a successful strawberry planting and an abysmal failure. He may be overdramatizing a little, but mulch can be very helpful. The nicest thing about mulching strawberries is that the mulch keeps the fruit clean.

Strawberries can be mulched right after planting. Chopped hay or straw is the mulch most frequently recommended.

Strawberries can be mulched right after planting. Chopped hay or straw is most frequently used. Some like to use sawdust or grass clippings. Apply 3 inches of straw and only 1 inch of sawdust or grass. Be careful not to cover the strawberry leaves with the mulch. A lot of folks are using black plastic around their strawberries. Of course, this is better applied before planting.

Winter mulching is essential to successful strawberry growing. It not only prevents heaving, which breaks roots, but protects the vulnerable crown of each plant, which is in real danger in temperatures below 10 degrees F. The plants should be protected by several inches of mulch whenever temperatures stay below 20 degrees F. for any extended period of time. In this part of the country, that would be somewhere between Thanksgiving and the middle of December.

Don't mulch your strawberry plants before that — early mulching can do more harm than not mulching at all. Covering your plants too soon will block sunlight from the leaves and halt photosynthesis. This will prevent the plants from producing and storing enough carbohydrates to get through the winter.

Straw is generally the mulch of choice for winter protection, but some work at Cornell University shows that row covers might also do the trick. Marvin Pritts, Assistant Professor with Cornell University's Pomology Department, explains that row covers even have a few advantages over straw: "Unlike straw, they are lightweight, easy to handle, weed-free, and do not delay bloom. Some are even biodegradable. In addition, they allow light to penetrate in the spring, resulting in higher yield."

He recommends removing the row covers before the plants start flowering or they may block pollination and increase the plants' susceptibility to botrytis fruit rot.

If you use one of the organic mulches, uncover the plants in late spring, when the new growth is about 2 inches long. Again, don't be overanxious. An early spring frost can nip off uncovered strawberry flowers, and you'll end up with fewer berries. As you remove the mulch, put half of it in the pathways between rows and leave the other half for the plants to grow through.

Raspberries and Blackberries

Although mulching is not necessary for either, according to Dr. Pritts, it will improve yields and lessen cold injury. He cautions against applying mulch too heavily, though. New growth may not be able to push through a thick layer.

You can mulch raspberries and blackberries almost immediately after planting. I use chopped hay or leaves or a combination of the two. Sawdust, wood chips, shavings, dried chopped cornstalks, and poultry litter can also be tried. Apply 3 or 4 inches to the row or over the entire soil surface. Be alert for nitrogen deficiencies.

Blueberries

Mulching blueberries can be a tricky thing. Some argue that they should not be mulched at all unless there is good soil drainage. Overmulching can make blueberries more susceptible to diseases. Other authorities admit that blueberries are apt to ripen later if they are mulched, but claim that higher yield is the end result.

Sawdust and chopped cornstalks are excellent mulches for blueberries. This resurrects the old myth about sawdust mulch "souring" the soil. Sawdust actually tends to influence the soil pH very little in most cases. But even if it were to make the soil more acidic, this would not hurt the blueberries. They seem to do best in a soil with a pH of 4.5 to 5.0, so they should never need lime. This means they can stand a permanent mulch, anywhere from 4 to 6 inches, of pine needles, peat moss, oak leaves, beech leaves, or other mulch that releases acid seepage. Black plastic, neither sweet nor sour, works well on blueberries, too.

Currants and Gooseberries

These two small fruits have experienced a resurgence in popularity over the last few years. Both will benefit from mulch's ability to keep soil temperatures down and moisture levels up. Just about any organic mulch will function around currants and gooseberries— straw, leaves, aged manure, sawdust, or whatever. Lay down 2 or 3 inches of these mulches while planting your bushes and replenish annually.

■ Chapter 9 ■

Here's How with Ornamentals

F irst, what is an ornamental? Well, for my purposes ornamentals include trees, shrubs, and bulbs not grown for their food value but for their visual contribution to the home landscape. Millions of dollars are spent by homeowners every year to add height, variety, and color to their front and back yards. Too often the critical step of mulching for healthier plants is skimped on or overlooked entirely.

As the interest and activity in home landscaping climbs, so does the demand for water to keep the plants alive. Forty percent of the water used in the United States is applied to outdoor landscapes. Without mulch a large portion of this water, some say as much as half, simply evaporates into thin air.

By including mulches in your landscape plan you're not only helping the water situation, but your trees and shrubs are happier, too. Mulching ornamentals will suppress weeds, regulate soil temperatures, add organic matter, and do all the other great things we have discussed throughout this book.

And since most landscape plantings are perennial in nature, you can use more permanent mulching techniques and materials. It's worth the time and effort to lay down a landscape fabric and cover it with lava rocks because you won't have to hassle with picking it up in the fall to plow.

Trees and Shrubs

With one or two exceptions, mulching trees and shrubs follows many of the same principles as mulching a vegetable garden or fruit

93

planting. Remove any existing weeds first and be sure the ground is well watered before applying a mulch. Don't overapply any material, and pick the best mulch for your situation. Simple rules to live by to get the most out of your mulching experience.

Probably the number-one cause of death for newly planted trees and shrubs is the lack of adequate water. We already know that mulching can help tackle that problem. I'd say the second leading cause of death (although I have not done or seen any research to back this up) is lawn mower damage.

You know how it is. You're cruising along on your riding mower and cut it just a bit too close to the honey locust tree. Off flies a chunk of bark. While one or two of these weekend collisions won't usually knock a tree out, enough of these bumps and bruises will damage the cambium and the tree will die. Not only that, open wounds in the bark can expose a plant to a number of disease and insect problems.

A good covering of mulch, say 3 inches deep, right after planting will go a long way toward protecting the base of your trees. It will suppress the weeds and grass surrounding your trees and help you resist the urge to mow right up to the trunk of your trees.

Wood chips, shredded bark or nuggets, cocoa hulls, pine needles, and nonpacking leaves are all smart choices for mulching trees or shrubs. Crushed stone, marble chips, and gravel can also be used, but these won't feed the soil and may not be as attractive to some. You'll want to be careful when applying any of the rock-type mulches around woody plants. They can do serious damage to woody plants if they hit the base of the tree.

For those of you who really want to make a statement with your mulch, look for one of the new decorative mulches made of "mineralized wood." I'm not sure what "mineralized" means, but it looks as though wood chips have been sprayed with something to give them some color and durability. These are recommended for use with the nonwoven geotextiles and come in all kinds of wild colors: green, red, brown, and "honey" are a few examples.

If the mulch around your trees doesn't seem as colorful as it was last year, don't just run out and add a whole new 3 inches of mulch. Check it out first. Maybe a light raking with the leaf rake or pitchfork will fluff it up and give it that fresh new feeling. If you're really lazy, I know the professional landscapers have a liquid concentrate called

Mulch-Magic, which they just spray on fibrous mulches to give them a shot in the arm. Maybe you could weasel a little to brighten up your wood chips.

If it does seem as though you need to add more mulch because yours has decomposed, add no more than you actually need. With wood chips you shouldn't need more than an inch or so. If you used chopped leaves or compost, you might need two or three inches. If maintaining bark chips or raking crushed stone out of the lawn is not for you, try one of the living mulches. Ground covers like ivy, periwinkle, or pachysandra can fulfill most of the requirements of a good landscape mulch, and they won't need mowing either.

There seem to be two shrubs that give people fits when it comes to mulching: rhododendrons and roses. While I can somewhat understand roses causing problems because of their demand for winter protection, I'm not sure why rhododendrons do. I guess it's due to the fact that we grow rhododendrons and azaleas for their spectacular bloom and when we don't get one, we want to blame something. Often, we blame the mulch.

Rhododendrons and Azaleas

Unmulched rhododendrons and azaleas, or those with an insufficient amount of mulch, may suffer from chlorosis, weak and underdeveloped leaves, or even death. These plants cannot tolerate hot, dry soil. Their feeding roots are severely injured under these conditions and the plant has trouble putting out healthy leaves, never mind spectacular blooms. Mulching can help cool the roots and hold the moisture.

In addition, since these are mostly evergreen plants, which carry their leaves all winter, they are continually losing water to the air. If there is an inadequate amount of soil moisture the plant will lose water faster than it can replace it. The end result will be brown, scorched foliage, which in extreme cases may just give up the ghost and drop off. By watering the ground well and mulching rhododendrons in the fall, you can ensure an ample moisture supply and insulate the soil from sudden temperature changes.

Rhododendrons and azaleas both prefer slightly acid soils, and your mulch selection can play a part. I suggest you choose one of the organic mulches, like leaves or pine needles. A dry leaf mulch (especially oak leaves), spread 10 to 12 inches deep, can be laid down at planting (remember, these will decompose quickly to give you a 3- or 4-inch layer). A 2- or 3-inch layer of pine needles will also do the trick. Wood chips or sawdust, if they are weathered, or peat moss can be substituted for pine needles.

If you are using one of these mulches, are watering your rhododendrons following a fertilizer schedule, and still have an unhealthy-looking plant, there must be something else going on. Maybe you have an insect or disease problem or grew the wrong variety for your part of the country. But let's not blame the mulch. It has a bad enough rap as it is.

Roses

Rose mulching offers a shining example of the differences between winter and summer mulches. Winter mulches, put down after the ground has started to cool down in the fall, will protect the plant from temperature extremes and heaving. Summer mulching is done in the spring to control weeds and maintain soil moisture.

Just about everyone who grows roses agrees that winter mulching is necessary to protect their plants. They don't always agree on *how* to do it but will concede that it is required. Winter mulching is fairly simple if you remember why you are doing it. Most roses are amazingly hardy. Mulch isn't meant to keep them from freezing: the goal is to maintain constant temperature and avoid freezing and thawing repeatedly.

There are hundreds of methods and materials for winterizing roses—almost as many as there are rose growers. Probably the most accepted is to take soil from somewhere else in the garden and make a mound of about 10 to 12 inches around the base of the rose bush. This should not be done until after the first hard frost. If it's done too early, the roses may be fooled into a late growth spurt, which will delay dormancy and lead to more winter injury, not less.

What you decide to do from this point opens up all kinds of possibilities. In areas where the temperature stays well below freezing for most of the season, you will want to provide some additional protection. Some lean toward the Styrofoam rose cones that fit around the mounds; others prefer ground corncobs, sawdust, or chopped leaves.

The rose cones work well when used in conjunction with the soil. They can overheat during those warm, sunny January thaws so it's a good idea to poke a ventilation hole in the top. Another suggestion

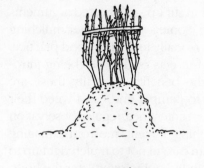

Mound soil at least 8 inches over each bush.

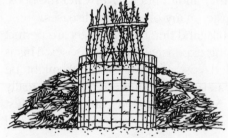

A cylinder of wire mesh holds mounded soil in place around canes.

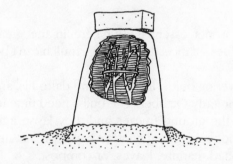

Styrofoam rose cones are held in place with a brick.

is to weight the cone down with a stone or something; otherwise your rose cone may end up in the neighbor's yard.

Wire cages filled with leaves or compost are often used in lieu of the Styrofoam cones. These cages needn't be stuffed to the gills with leaves. This makes for poor air circulation and may lead to disease problems.

Whichever system you select, water the soil well before covering your roses and remove the mulch in the spring before new growth begins. If the mulch is left on until the buds start swelling, it may put the new growth into shock when you uncover it.

Among true rosarians nothing can stir up such heated arguments as the subject of summer mulching. Some swear summer mulching is a must, but others swear at it. I personally feel it is a good practice.

Anti-mulchers feel the threat of insects or diseases being introduced with a mulch outweighs the benefits. Usually these are dedicated growers who have time to pamper and hand-weed their rose beds weekly. I opt for the lower-maintenance, regular-observation method. For amateurs like me, mulching prevents me from damaging shallow roots during cultivation. I am careful not to mulch right up to the base of my bushes, and I am mindful not to overwater the beds. Moist, damp conditions can foster many of the rose diseases.

Buckwheat hulls, cocoa hulls, and fine bark nuggets are perfect summer mulches for showcasing expensive specimen roses. This is one instance where the added cost of these mulches might be justified. The dark, rich colors associated with these types can really accent an already impressive rose display. Corncobs and sawdust may also be utilized, but you will have to supplement the soil nitrogen.

Bulbs

Certainly, mulching bulbs is not essential. But here in the great Northeast, the insulating value of a nice, thick organic mulch can't be overlooked.

In Vermont, spring-flowering bulbs, like tulips and daffodils, are planted in late September or early October. The bulbs need time to develop their roots before the ground freezes and they lapse into winter dormancy. To postpone their long winter's nap, I protect my plantings with a layer of rotted manure, leaves, or compost.

Wood chips, corncobs, sawdust—just about any mulch will be fine for bulbs. Don't worry about the weight of the mulch inhibiting the emergence of your bulbs. If they can push up through a wet, spring soil or several inches of snow, I doubt a couple of inches of mulch will slow them down.

Epilogue

I t took me twenty-seven years to recover from those boring hot days in my mother's garden and to recover some of the wonder I see written all over my daughter's face when she looks at growing things. If anyone had told me several years ago that today I would be a "gardening freak," I would have acknowledged the prediction with a cynical chuckle.

No one could have convinced me that freshly tilled soil is as beautiful as new snow on the top of Mt. Mansfield, or that the first radish of the season is as exciting as sailing on Lake Champlain in a strong north wind. I know better now, but an earlier me would be shocked to see me now—that man who sits motionless in the garden for long periods watching and worrying, and planning how it is going to be better next year.

It's all because an elderly writer and organic gardening authority by the name of Sam Ogden sensed my conviction that I had a black thumb one day when I visited him in Landgrove, Vermont. "Plants aren't as fragile as you think they are," he said as he led me into his huge and immaculate garden. "Don't be afraid."

For me, through his bushy white mustache, he reduced man's fascination with plants to the simplest possible terms. "The real beauty of gardening," he said, "is in the knowledge that when you plant seed in the spring something is going to happen. Germination is an annual miracle that never fails to repeat itself."

The most comforting thing about gardening is that no one, not even a lifelong expert like Sam Ogden, has all the answers. I hope that I have not left too many questions about mulching unanswered. But any gardener who claims to know it all should be drummed out of the gardening corps—not because he is a know-it-all, but because somewhere along the line he has lost that sense of mystery, that feeling of humble uncertainty that all gardeners should have.

The botanical scientists and horticultural experimenters *must* keep on with their good work. They must continue to give us direction and reduce as much as possible the chances of us failing with our gardens.

But happily, because there are so many variables in gardening, because it is so very difficult to duplicate tightly controlled laboratory conditions outdoors, because all of the enemy elements refuse to be cataloged and thwarted, it should be a century or two before the scientists can tell us everything. Even then it is doubtful that Mother Nature will allow herself to be regulated altogether.

So if this generation, or even the next, has trouble distinguishing between scientific *fact* and old wives' remedies that seem to work in the garden, no one should worry about it too much. Once all the question marks are erased, once all the mysteries have been solved, gardening may not be so much fun anymore. Keep the faith.

A few evenings ago my three-year-old came into the garden again, of her own accord. She wanted to help, and I didn't want to let her go again, so we did some simple jobs together. We laid walkways of hay mulch between rows of vegetables. We tucked chopped hay around cabbage plants. We sprinkled chopped leaves around onion tops, and planted more string beans under mulch. Her stubby fingers did just fine. She asked questions and I did my best to answer. Often I said, "I don't know."

And last night she was waiting outside the door to greet me when I came home. "Come on," she said, and took me by the hand. She led me past the pen without even a glance at the ten puppies inside, and took me into the garden. She led me expertly through a labyrinth of walkways, avoiding places where things we couldn't see were growing under mulch. She showed me how a pepper with a pointed bottom was turning red. She showed *me* where a precocious Kentucky Wonder pole bean tendril had wound its way to the top of its pole and beyond, heavenward. Standing there, holding my daughter's hand, I was awestruck by the symbolism of the moment. Who says the chances for a greener, happier, more peaceful world are out of reach?

Quick-Reference Chart

MULCH MATERIALS

Material	Appearance	Insulation Value	Relative Cost	Thickness	Weed Control
Aluminum foil	Poor	Fair; reflects sun's heat	Very high	1 layer	Good
Asphalt	Poor	Fair	High	½–1 in.	Fair
Bark, mixed	Good	Good	Moderate	2–3 in.	Good
Bark, redwood	Excellent	Good	High	2–3 in.	Fair
Buckwheat hulls	Good	Good	High	1–1½ in.	Good; may sprout
Burlap	Poor	Fair	Moderate	1 layer or more	Poor
Cocoa hulls	Good–excellent	Good; absorbs heat from sun	High in most areas	1 in.	Good
Coffee grounds	Good	Fair	Low but not plentiful	Never more than 1 in.	Good
Compost	Fair	Good	High; supply usually limited	1–3 in.	Good
Cork, ground	Fair–good	Excellent	High	1–2 in.	Good
Corncobs, ground	Good	Good	Low in Midwest	2–3 in.	Excellent
Cottonseed hulls	Good	Good	Low in the South	1–2 in.	Good
Cranberry vines	Good	Fair	Low in some areas	3–4 in., 2 in. if chopped	Fair–good

Water Penetration	Soil Moisture Retention	Decomposition Speed	Comments
Poor, unless perforated	Excellent	No decomposition	Aphids shy away from foil-mulched plants. Should be removed and recycled.
Fair	Fair–good	Decomposes in about 1 year	Complicated for home gardener to apply.
Good	Good	Slow unless composted before use	Must be replaced only every two years. Can be stringy, difficult to manage.
Fair; repels water in some places	Fair	Very slow; add nitrogen to application	Earthworms avoid redwood. May act as an insect repellent.
Excellent	Fair	Slow	Easy to handle. May be blown around in high wind or splashed by rain.
Excellent	Fair	Slow	Excellent for preventing erosion on slopes. New grass grows right through it.
Good unless allowed to mat	Good	Slow; adds nitrogen to soil	Sawdust can be added to improve texture and increase water retention. May develop mold. Has chocolatey smell.
Fair; may cake	Good	Fairly rapid	Use carefully. May prevent ventilation. Best used in container gardens.
Good if well rotted	Good	Rapid; adds nutrients	Partially decomposed compost is an excellent feeding mulch.
Good	Good	Very slow; has little effect on soil nitrogen	Odorless. Stays in place nicely once it has been soaked.
Fair; should be well soaked before applying	Excellent	Nitrogen fertilizer should be added	Avoid close contact with stems of plants because of heat generation.
Good	Good	Fairly rapid	Will blow in wind. Has fertilizer value similar to cottonseed meal.
Good	Good	Fairly rapid	Excellent winter cover mulch. Pea vines have similar characteristics.

continued

Mulch Materials (continued)

Material	Appearance	Insulation Value	Relative Cost	Thickness	Weed Control
Evergreen boughs	Poor	Good; recommended for wind protection	Low	1 to several layers	Fair
Felt paper (tar paper)	Poor	Good; absorbs heat from sun	High	1 layer	Excellent
Fiberglass	Poor	Excellent	High	3½–6 in.	Excellent
Grass clippings	Poor if not dried. Can have unpleasant odor.	Good	Low	1 in. maximum	Fair
Geotextiles	Poor, without a cover mulch	Poor	High	Single layer	Good
Green ground covers (cover crops)	Fair	Good once there is a heavy sod	Low	Allow to grow to full height	Good
Growing green mulch	Excellent	Fair	Moderate	1 layer	Fair
Hay	Poor unless chopped	Good	Low, if spoiled	6–8 in., 2–3 in. if chopped	Good
Hops, spent	Fair	Fair; heats up when wet	Low where available	1–3 in.	Good
Leaves	Fair	Good	Low	4–6 in.	Good
Leaf mold	Fair	Good	Low	1½ in.	Fair–good
Manure	Poor–fair	Good	Moderate–high	As thick as supply allows	Fair

Water Penetration	Soil Moisture Retention	Decomposition Speed	Comments
Good	Fair	Slow	Good for erosion control. Should be removed from perennials in spring.
Poor, unless perforated	Good	Extremely slow if at all	Difficult to manage, tears. Must be carefully weighted and removed each fall.
Fair; will get soggy and mat	Good	No decomposition	Unpleasant to handle. Totally fireproof. Mats are better than building insulation.
Good if not matted	Fair	Rapid; green grass adds nitrogen	Can be mixed with peat moss. After drying can be spread thinly around young plants.
Fair	Good	Rapid with exposure to sunlight; slower with use of cover mulch	Use of a cover mulch highly recommended.
Good	Good	Decomposing legumes and cover crops are rich in nitrogen	Should be harvested or tilled directly into the soil.
Good	Good	Will live from one year to the next	Includes myrtle, pachysandra, etc. Use where you are not going to walk.
Good	Good	Rapid; adds nitrogen	Second- or third-growth hay that has not gone to seed is ideal.
Good	Good	Slow; rich in nitrogen and other nutrients	Avoid close contact with trunks and stems because of heating.
Fair; likely to mat	Good	Fairly slow; adds nitrogen	Contributes many valuable nutrients. Can be chopped and mixed with other things.
Fair; prevents percolation if too thick	Good	Rapid	An excellent feeding mulch. Use like compost.
Fair–good	Good	Rapid; adds nitrogen; packaged mixes may have harmful salts	Should be at least partially rotted. Supplies many nutrients.

continued

MULCH MATERIALS (CONTINUED)

Material	Appearance	Insulation Value	Relative Cost	Thickness	Weed Control
Muck	Poor	Fair	Moderate	1–2 in.	Fair
Oak leaf mulch	Good	Good	Low	2–4 in.	Good
Oyster shells, ground	Good	Fair	High	1–2 in.	Fair
Paper	Poor; can be covered with soil	Fair	Low, but specialized mulch paper is expensive	1–several layers	Good
Paper pulp	Poor	Fair	Moderate	½ in.	Fair
Peanut hulls	Good	Good	Low where plentiful	1–2 in.	Good
Peat moss	Good	Good	Moderate–high	1 in.	Good
Pine needles	Good–excellent	Good	Low	1–1½ in.	Good
Plastic	Poor, but can be covered	Fair; some colors absorb heat	Moderate–high	1–6 mil.	Excellent
Poultry litter	Poor	Fair	Low–moderate	½ in.	Fair
Pyrophyllite	Fair	Fair	High	1–3 in.	Fair
Salt hay	Good	Good	Moderate, unless you gather it yourself	3–6 in.	Good; contains no seed
Sawdust	Fair–good	Good	Low	1–1½ in.	Good

Water Penetration	Soil Moisture Retention	Decomposition Speed	Comments
Good, but will splash and wash away	Fair	Rapid	Very fertile. Can be mixed with other materials to improve texture.
Good	Good	Slow	Recommended for acid-soil plants. Has only slight influence on soil pH.
Good	Good	Slow	Works like lime. Will raise soil pH.
Poor unless perforated	Good	Slow, unless designed to be biodegradable	Can be shredded and used effectively.
Fair	Good	Rapid, nitrogen-rich as side-dressing	Requires special equipment. Useful in deep-planting operations. Good way to recycle.
Good	Good	Rapid; adds nitrogen	Can be mixed with other material for superior appearance. Might splash in rain.
Poor; absorbs much water	Poor; draws moisture from soil	Very slow	Adds little or no nutrients to soil. Valuable only as a soil conditioner.
Excellent	Good	Slow; very little earthworm activity	Often used with acid-soil plants, but can be used elsewhere.
Poor unless perforated	Excellent	No decomposition	Contributes nothing to the soil. Must be handled twice a year. Various colors available.
Good	Fair	Very rapid; adds nitrogen	Should not be used unless mixed with dry material. Excellent fertilizer.
Good	Fair	Extremely slow	Should be considered a permanent mulch.
Good, does not mat	Good	Slow	Can be used year after year. Is pest-free. Good for winter protection.
Fair	Fair	Slow unless weathered; robs soil nitrogen	Has high carbon content. Does not sour soil. Very little earthworm activity.

continued

Mulch Materials (continued)

Material	Appearance	Insulation Value	Relative Cost	Thickness	Weed Control
Seaweed (kelp)	Poor	Good; recommended as a winter mulch	Low in coastal areas	4–6 in.	Excellent
Stone	Excellent	Good; dark stone retains heat, light stone reflects	High	2–4 in.	Fair, except shale
Straw	Fair, unless chopped	Good	Low–moderate	6–8 in., 1–2 in. if chopped	Good; avoid oat straw for weed control
Sugarcane (bagasse)	Poor–fair	Good	Moderate	2–3 in.	Good
Vermiculite	Excellent	Excellent	High	½ in.	Good
Walnut shells	Excellent	Good	Low where plentiful	1–2 in.	Good
Wood chips	Good	Good	Moderate	2–4 in.	Good
Wood shavings	Fair	Fair	Low	2–3 in.	Fair

Water Penetration	Soil Moisture Retention	Decomposition Speed	Comments
Fair	Good	Slow; adds nitrogen and potash	Provides sodium, boron, and other trace elements. Excellent for sheet composting.
Good	Fair	Extremely slow	Should be considered permanent mulch. Contributes some trace elements through leaching.
Good	Good	Fairly slow; nitrogen fertilizer is helpful	Should be seed-free if possible. Straw is highly flammable.
Good	Good	Rapid due to sugar content	Needs to be replenished often. Has fairly low pH. Mix with lime.
Good	Good	Extremely slow	Totally sterile. Recommended for hothouse use. Will blow and splash outdoors.
Good	Good	Very slow	Will furnish good trace elements. Resists fire.
Good	Good	Fairly slow; little effect on soil nitrogen	May contain carpenter ants, but does not retain tree diseases.
Good	Fair	Very rapid; will use up soil nitrogen	Hardwood shavings are better than pine or spruce. Chips or sawdust make better mulch.

AMOUNT OF ORGANIC MATERIAL NEEDED
TO COVER 100 SQUARE FOOT AREA

Inches of organic material	Material needed to cover 100 sq. ft.
6"	2 cubic yards
4"	35 cubic feet
3"	1 cubic yard
2"	18 cubic feet
1"	9 cubic feet
½"	4 cubic feet
¼"	2 cubic feet

1 cubic yard = 27 cubic feet

Source: Joann Gruttardio, Plant Science, Cornell University.

End Notes

1. Ruth Stout and Richard Clemence, *The Ruth Stout No-work Garden Book,* p. 2.
2. Ibid, pp. 3-4.
3. From Ruth Stout, *How to Have a Green Thumb without an Aching Back.*
4. *The Ruth Stout No-work Garden Book,* p. 119.
5. Leonard Wickenden, *Gardening with Nature,* pp. 47-48.
6. Ruth Stout, *Gardening without Work,* pp. 197-198.
7. John and Helen Philbrick, *The Bug Book: Harmless Insect Controls,* p. 107.
8. Robert Rodale, Ed., *The Basic Book of Organic Gardening,* pp. 76-77.
9. Arno and Irene Nehrling, *Easy Gardening with Drought Resistant Plants,* p. 92.
10. Rodale et al., p. 147.
11. Albert C. Burrage, *Burrage on Vegetables,* p. 121.
12. *The Ruth Stout No-work Garden Book,* pp. 16-17.
13. Josephine Neuse, *The Country Gardener,* p. 44.
14. From Chuck Pendergast, *Introduction to Organic Gardening.*
15. Helen and John Philbrick, *The Bug Book,* p. 107.
16. Dr. Pfeiffer is quoted in John and Helen Philbrick, *Gardening for Health and Nutrition,* p. 69.

Bibliography

Burrage, Albert. *Burrage on Vegetables*. New York: Van Nostrand, 1954.

Cruso, Thalassa. *Making Things Grow Outdoors*. New York: Alfred A. Knopf, 1971.

Flanagan, Ted. "Plastic Mulch." *The Green Mountain Gardener,* University of Vermont, 1969.

Foster, Catherine Osgood. *Building Healthy Gardens*. Pownal, Vermont: Garden Way Publishing, 1988.

Foulds, Raymond, Jr. "Mulching." University of Vermont, 1973.

Hopp, Henry. *What Every Gardener Should Know about Earthworms*. Garden Way Publishing Bulletin #21, Pownal, Vermont, 1978.

Hull, George F. *The Know-Nothing Gardener's Guide to Success*. New York: Hawthorne, 1969.

Hunter, Beatrice Trum. *Gardening without Poisons*. Boston: Houghton Mifflin, 1971.

Kiplinger, D. C., Brooks, W. M., Utzinger, J. D., Tayama, Harry K. "Mulches for Home Grounds." Ohio State University, 1970.

Langer, Richard W. *Grow It!* New York: Saturday Review Press, 1972.

"Mulching Vegetables: Practices and Commercial Applications." University of Illinois, 1969.

Nuese, Josephine. *The Country Garden*. New York: Charles Scribner's Sons, 1970; rev. ed. 1987.

Ourecky, D.K. and Tomkins, J.P. *Raspberry Growing in New York State*. Cornell University, 1971.

Pendergast, Chuck. *Introduction to Organic Gardening.* Los Angeles, Nash Publishing, 1970.

Philbrick, John and Helen. *The Bug Book: Harmless Insect Controls.* Pownal, Vermont: Garden Way Publishing, 1974.

Philbrick, John and Helen. *Gardening for Health and Nutrition.* New York: Harper and Row, 1980.

Pritts, Marvin and Handley, David. *Bramble Production Guide.* Ithaca, New York: Northeast Regional Agricultural Engineering Service, 1989.

Rakow, Donald. *Types and Uses of Mulch in the Landscape.* Cornell University, 1989.

Rodale, Robert (ed.) and staff, *The Organic Way to Mulching.* Emmaus, Pennsylvania: Rodale Press, 1972.

Shutak, V. G. and Christopher, E. P. *Sawdust Mulch for Blueberries.* University of Rhode Island, 1952.

Southwick, Lawrence. *Planting Your Dwarf Fruit Orchard.* Garden Way Publishing Bulletin #8, Pownal, Vermont, 1977.

Stout, Ruth. *Gardening without Work.* Old Greenwich, Connecticut: Devin-Adair, 1961.

Stout, Ruth. *How to Have a Green Thumb without an Aching Back.* New York: Exposition Press, 1968.

Stout, Ruth and Clemence, Richard, *The Ruth Stout No-Work Garden Book.* Emmaus, Pennsylvania: Rodale Press, 1971.

Thies, W. H. *Growing Fruits for Home Use.* University of Massachusetts, 1952.

Wells, Ortho S. *Mulching with Black Plastic in the Home Garden.* University of New Hampshire, 1971.

Wickenden, Leonard. *Gardening with Nature.* Old Greenwich, Connecticut: Devin- Adair, 1954; rev. ed 1972.

Wyman, Donald. *The Saturday Morning Gardener.* New York: Macmillan, 1962.

Where to Find Mulching Supplies

Your local nursery or garden center is likely to carry a variety of mulching products. To order by mail, or to obtain product information, consult the companies listed below.

This is only a partial listing. *The Complete Guide to Gardening by Mail* is available from The Mailorder Association of Nurseries, Dept. SCI, 8683 Doves Fly Way, Laurel, MD 20723. Please add $1.00 for postage and handling.

Chippers/Shredders

Garden Way Manufacturing, Inc.
102nd Street & 9th Avenue
Troy, NY 12180

Kemp Company
160 Koser Road
Lititz, PA 17543

John Deere Catalog
1400 Third Avenue
Moline, IL 61265

Mantis Manufacturing
1458 County Line Road
Huntingdon Valley, PA 19006

Landscape Fabrics

DeWitt Company, Inc.
85 DeWitt Drive
Sikeston, MO 63801

Easy Gardener
P.O. Box 21025
Waco, TX 76702

K.I.M. International
6433 Warren Drive
Norcross, GA 30093

Reemay, Inc.
P.O. Box 511
70 Old Hickory
Old Hickory, TN 37138

General Gardening Supplies

Alsto's Handy Helpers
P.O. Box 1267
Galesberg, IL 61401

Earl May Seed & Nursery
208 North Elm Street
Shenandoah, IA 51603

Gardener's Supply
128 Intervale Road
Burlington, VT 05401

Gurney Seed & Nursery
110 Capital Street
Yankton, SD 57078

H.G. Hasting Co.
3920 Peach Tree Road
Atlanta, GA 30310

Henry Fields
415 North Burnett
Shenandoah, IA 51602

Johnny's Selected Seed
310 Foss Hill Road
Albion, ME 04910

J.W. Jung Seed Co.
335 South High Street
Randolph, WI 53957

Kinsman Garden Company, Inc.
River Road
Point Pleasant, IA 18950

Mellinger's Inc.
2310 West South Range Road
North Lima, OH 44452

Modern Farm
1825 Big Horn Avenue
Cody, WY 82414

Natural Gardening Company
217 San Anselmo Avenue
San Anselmo, CA 94960

Natural Gardening Research Center
Gardens Alive! catalog
P.O. Box 149
Sunman, IN 47041

Necessary Trading Company
P.O. Box 305
422 Salem Avenue
New Castle, VA 24127

Peaceful Valley Farm Supply
P.O. Box 2209
Grass Valley, CA 95945

Pinetree Garden Seeds
Box 300
New Gloucester, ME 04260

Plow and Hearth
301 Madison Road
Orange, VA 22960

Ringer Corporation
9959 Valley View Road
Eden Prairie, MN 55344

Smith & Hawken
117 East Strawberry Drive
Mill Valley, CA 94941

The Walt Nicke Company
P.O. Box 443
36 McLeod Lane
Topsfield, MA 01983

Index

Page numbers in *italics* refer to illustrations and/or tables.

117

Mice, 21, 86, 88
Microbial activity, 9, 18
Mineralized wood, 94
Moisture conservation, 6, 47, 69, 89, 95-96. *See also* Soil moisture
Molds, 32, 63
Muck, 42, *106-107*
Mulch, 24, 59
    guidelines, 55-57, *61, 102-109*
        for fruits, 88-92
        for ornamentals, 93-98
        for vegetables, 67-81
Mulch-Magic, 95

N
Newspaper, 43-44
Nitrogen, 10, 15, 49, 91
    loss, 16, 19, 50, 60

O
Oak leaves, 42, 92, *106-107*
Odor, 57
Ogden, Sam, 99
Onions, 75
Organic mulches, 9, 24
Ornamentals, 25, 93-98
Oyster shells, 43, *106-107*

P
Pachysandra, 38
Paper, 26, 43-45, *44*, 78, *106-107*
Parsley, 76
Parsnips, 76-77, *76*
Pea vines, 78, 81
Peanut hulls, 45, *106-107*
Peas, 77-78, *77*
Peat moss, 19, 45-46, 92, *106-107*
Pendergast, Chuck, 85
Peppers, 78
Perennial weeds, 19
Perennials, 87. *See also* Fruits, Ornamentals
Permanent mulch, 27, 72-73, 92
Pfeiffer, Dr. D. E., 88
pH, 43, 47, 71, 91-92, 95
Philbrick, John and Helen, 42, 87

Phosphorus, 10
Pine needles, 46-47, *106-107*
    for berries, 92
    for ornamentals, 94, 95-96
Plastic mulch, 30, *60,* 63
Polyester, 24, 36
Polyethlene, 10, 47-48, 70, *106-107*
Polypropylene. *See* Geotextiles
Potassium, 10, 32
Potato bugs, 78-79
Potatoes, 78-79
Poultry litter, 49, *106-107*
Pritts, Marvin, 91
Pumpkins, 79
Pyrophyllite, 49, *106-107*

R
Radishes, 79
Rainfall, 5, 17-18
Rakow, Dr. Donald, 5, 10, 32
Raspberries, 91
Raymond, Dick, 31, 59, 68-69
Redwood chips, 31, *102-103*
Replacing mulch, 63, 94
Rhododendrons, 95-96
Rhubarb, 79
Rock gardens, 25
Rock mulch, 80
Rodale Press, 68, 71, 79
Rodents, 21, 86, 88
Root(s), 20, 53, 61, 63
    growth, 7-8, 9, 18
Roses, 96-98, *97*
Rutabagas, 69
Ryegrass, 25

S
Salt hay, 49, *106-107*
Sawdust, 19, 50, 60, *106-107*
    for fruits, 79, 88, 90, 91, 92
    for ornamentals, 96, 98
    for vegetables, 80
Seasonal changes, 59-60, 83-87
Seaweed, 50-51, 69-70, *108-109*
Seeds, 18, 62-63, *62,* 70
Sheet composting, 14, 16, 23